Shakespeare's
MISSING
YEARS

Shakespeare's
MISSING
YEARS

JOHN IDRIS JONES

FONTHILL

This work is dedicated to the memory of Dr Eric Sams,
for his encouragement, generosity, and friendship:
an extraordinary mind.

With grateful thanks to skilled publishers Alan Sutton,
Jay Slater, and Jamie Hardwick.

J. I. J.

Fonthill Media Language Policy

Fonthill Media publishes in the international English language market. One language edition is published worldwide. As there are minor differences in spelling and presentation, especially with regard to American English and British English, a policy is necessary to define which form of English to use. The Fonthill Policy is to use the form of English native to the author. John Idris Jones was born and educated in the United Kingdom; therefore, British English has been adopted in this publication.

Fonthill Media Limited
Fonthill Media LLC
www.fonthillmedia.com
office@fonthillmedia.com

First published in the United Kingdom and the United States of America 2018

British Library Cataloguing in Publication Data:
A catalogue record for this book is available from the British Library

Copyright © John Idris Jones 2018

ISBN 978-1-78155-676-4

Typeset in 10pt on 13pt Sabon
Printed by CPI Group (UK) Ltd, Croydon CR0 4YY

Preface

Who is this reader and quoter of Ovid, Plutarch and the Bible, this student, adapter and versifier of Holinshed and Grafton, this deliberate rhetorician, inventor of new vocabulary, compound-word-coiner, poet and punster (in Latin too), ardent alliterator, lover of classical and legal allusion, bawdy humorist, amused observer of low life, purveyor of comic relief and dramatic irony, this pioneer of a new genre with a new subject from a new source, this showman of theatrical spectacle, this originator of fresh imagery from the outdoor life of country pursuits and natural surroundings, from fables and proverbs and animal lore, with his curiously solecistic grammar, his eccentric scansion of proper names, his deliberate references to acting and the stage, his intense patriotism, his dread of civil war, his close concern with political stability and social status, his obsessive hatred of flattery, its association in his mind with the idea of sugar, melting and dogs, his further association of death with hollowness, and of blots with faces, the sky, constancy, coldness and kings, his persistent thinking in contrasts and antithesis—who can this possibly be?

from Eric Sams's Introduction (p. 5) to his *Shakespeare's 'Edmund Ironside'* (Wildwood House, 1986)

Why write I still all one, ever the same,
And keep invention in a noted weed,
That every word almost doth tell my name,
Showing their birth, and where they did proceed?

Shakespeare, *Sonnet 76*

The content of this book began to take shape in my mind when, in the early 1990s, I received a telephone call and written information from my friend

Tom Lloyd-Roberts of Denbigh. Tom had recently given up the business of antiquarian bookseller, working from nearby Caerwys, where he had spent his life in the company of old books—he was an expert on the history of Wales, especially the Tudor period. 'Had I thought of Shakespeare and Wales?' said Tom.

'Well,' I answered, 'I know of Henry Tudor, *Cymbeline*, Milford, and Flint Castle.'

'How did he know that Flint Castle had a plain around it?' he said. 'Had he been there? And there's this poem in the Salusbury Papers in Christ Church Library, Oxford; I think it's by Shakespeare. Would you like to have a look at it?'

He sent me the material, and that was the beginning of my personal research. Here is the greatest writer the world has ever seen, the son of an ordinary man living in provincial Stratford-upon-Avon, and we do not know where he was or what he was doing for almost all of the first third of his life. We know he was born in 1564 and he was christened in Stratford on 30 April 1564. We have no contemporary record—not even a mention in correspondence, bills of sale, receipts, etc.—of his existence in Stratford through his childhood or school days. His old school still stands, but the records from this period are long gone. We then know that he married Anne Hathaway in November 1582, when he was eighteen. There is a record of the christening of their first child in May 1583, some six months into his marriage. Then, after a gap of almost two years, there is a record of the birth of twins in February 1585. These are four events from his personal life, but we know practically nothing else of his early biography. We factually do not know the day of his birth; we do not know for sure which house or houses he lived in; we know nothing of the circumstances (family, friends, or household habits) of his upbringing; and we do not know for certain that he attended Stratford Grammar School, although he probably did.

From when he left school (possibly in 1578) to early 1592, there is a gap in what we know of his life. When you would expect that a life would be varied, busy, explorative, and colourful, corroborated by some preserved detail or reference, we have not a single reliable indication of his whereabouts and activities. You would expect an able young man, living in a crowded house in a market town, to leave home and strike out—but did he? Nothing tells us that he was in Stratford after his school years, and we do not know that he was anywhere else. We have to rely on presumption if we want to try to solve the mystery of the 'missing years'.

Robin Reeves, the then editor of *The New Welsh Review*, asked Tom to prepare his material for publication in that periodical. It was published in edition No. 23, Winter 1993–4, with the title 'Bard of Lleweni? Shakespeare's Welsh connection'. In the contents, the editor wrote:

After studying Wales's Elizabethan history for 30 years Tom Lloyd-Roberts calculates William Shakespeare not only stayed in north Wales with friend and patron Sir John Salusbury during the winter of 1593–4—exactly 400 years ago—but that he also wrote some verses in the Lleweni manuscript, reproduced here. In an exclusive article, he explains why.

... examples of Shakespeare's handwriting beyond the signature on his will are rare and unproven. This makes the results of Tom Lloyd-Roberts's Elizabethan researches and Shakespeare's Welsh connection all the more intriguing. If he is right, he has not only discovered some previously unrecognised Shakespeare verses but verses written in Shakespeare's own hand early in his career. In the best traditions of historical research, Mr Lloyd-Roberts is not claiming this as fact but as a possibility. He has asked Christ Church, Oxford, to arrange for the relevant Lleweni manuscripts in its possession to be examined scientifically. His request should be acted upon.

Christ Church Library did subject the MSS to some tests, which were unsuccessful.

Tom Lloyd-Roberts and Robin Reeves have passed away. I owe them a debt of gratitude; they opened a subject that has invigorated my life. This book is a tribute to them. It continues the work that Tom started, and it would not exist were it not for his scholarship and insight.

The New Welsh Review published the Christ Church verses: twelve six-line stanzas under 'XXI' and five following stanzas under 'XXII'. They printed them exactly as they are printed in the Carleton Brown volume (more of which later).

Robin Reeves then asked me to work on them. Could they be by Shakespeare, as Tom alleged? I started very sceptically. Stories of 'new' work by Shakespeare had appeared in the press and the journals and none of them had been reliable. Yet as I ploughed on, through volumes of literary criticism, commentary, and reference (I had retired from full-time teaching by this time), following the slightest trails, I began to think that this could be Shakespeare's work. Certainly, there was nothing in the untitled poem (I was now calling it 'The Denbigh Poem') that made it certain that it was not the work of Shakespeare. My results (along with a good reproduction of the original handwritten manuscript) appeared in *The New Welsh Review*, No. 25, Summer 1994, under the title, 'The Structure of *Venus and Adonis*, the Spirit of *A Midsummer Night's Dream*, the Case in Favour'. Some of the views expressed in that essay have since been modified and altered, but the general gist of it I hold now.

The Times printed a reproduction of part of the Denbigh Poem manuscript. I received a letter from Eric Sams; he said the handwriting looked very like the hand of the marginal notes in *The Annotator*, a book by Alan Keen and Roger Lubbock. Dr Sams sent me a copy of the book, which has been invaluable. He does not go in to the Lancashire Theory (which is the theory that William

Shakespeare spent part of his younger days with Catholic families in Lancashire) in his books and articles (understandably, because of its speculative nature). However, I asked him directly one day, on the telephone, 'Eric, do you think the Lancashire Theory is true?' He replied without hesitation, 'Yes, I think it is very possible.' The words 'very possible' have stayed in my mind (spoken by one awarded a Cambridge doctorate and one of the world's leading experts on the life of Shakespeare) throughout my investigations. Eric has since passed away. The dozens of letters I received from him have been copied by Erik Battaglia and are available on the Sams Shakespeare website. I gave the originals to the Shakespeare Memorial Library, Stratford-upon-Avon.

My research broadened and Shakespeare, Lancashire, and the Stanleys became my subject. For if Shakespeare might have been in Denbigh, north-east Wales, during Christmas 1593 and the beginning of 1594, it would be linked with the family of Ursula (Stanley), John Salusbury's wife, and to her father Henry, the Fourth Earl of Derby, whose main residences were Knowsley (now in Merseyside) and, principally, Lathom (near Ormskirk, Lancashire), now non-existent above ground. It would especially have a link with Ursula's half-brother Ferdinando, who became the Fifth Earl in September 1593. He was a patron of writers and under him, the playing group that eventually became The Chamberlain's Men was born.

I owe special thanks to Emeritus Professor Leo Daugherty of Charlottesville, Virginia. I met him at a conference on Shakespeare in Lancashire at the University of Lancaster. I shall quote part of his letter to me:

> Since last writing you, I had the weird and wonderful coincidence of coming upon this copy of Brown's *POEMS OF SALUSBURIE AND CHESTER*— this just as I was getting ready to Xerox a copy to you. Although it's rare, I got it for a song, and I'm hoping that you'll accept it as the proverbial token of my esteem—because that's precisely what it is. You of all people need a complete copy of this book to work from, and I have two copies here at the Univ. of Virginia library (one of the best in the States, thankfully) and so I don't need it at all.

Thirdly, I wish to record my admiration and respect for the work of Prof E. A. J. Honigmann, whose *Shakespeare: The 'Lost Years'* (Manchester University Press, 1985) is essential reading for anybody interested in the Lancashire Theory. I value his letters and his comment, 'Please send me your new research papers' a few weeks before he passed away.

If the whole life of Shakespeare was depicted pictorially on a jigsaw of say a hundred pieces, each one representing what we know, the pieces making up the period 1592–1616 would be about two-thirds complete, and the biographical picture in that section would be reasonably clear. However, the section representing the period April 1564 (when he was born) to March 1592 (when his first plays were performed on the public stage in London) would be 90 per cent missing, and no overall representation would present itself. The aim of this book is to present to the reader what might well be some of the pieces in that section, so that a clearer picture of the first third of the life might emerge. It is a journey of discovery, something like a detective story. I shall present the material. The reader will decide what to believe in.

CONTENTS

Introduction

For an enthusiast, it is the most important book ever published. William Shakespeare's 'collected plays' first appeared on booksellers' tables in London in the autumn of 1623. It was a large volume, originally unbound, measuring some 13 inches high by 8 inches across, 2 inches thick. Sir Edward Dering recorded the purchase of two copies for £2 in 5 December 1623. The records do not tell us how many copies were printed of the first edition—perhaps, according to Halliday, about 1,000. Most of these have disappeared over the last 400 years, but approximately 232 remain. Eighty-two of these are in the Folger Shakespeare Library, Washington D.C., USA, where they lie on shelves in an underground vault.

The volume's title page is taken up by an engraving of the author. Above this appear the words: 'Mr. WILLIAM/SHAKESPEARES/COMEDIES,/HISTORIES, &/TRAGEDIES./Published according to the True Originall [sic] Copies.' 'To the great Variety of Readers', an address to the reader by editors John Heminge and Henry Condell on page seven, tells us that this was a book for a 'variety' of readers, meaning not just for the elite. This hints at the author's ability to reach those in different parts of society.

The first edition of the First Folio, as it has come to be called, contained thirty-six of Shakespeare's plays. Of these, eighteen had already been published individually. The Folio contains eighteen unpublished plays. It has two columns of 'Principall [sic] Actors'; of the twenty-six, the first are: 'William Shakespeare, Richard Burbadge, John Hemmings, Augustine Phillips, William Kempt, Thomas Poope, George Bryan, Henry Condell, William Sly.' This is a significant list; it tells us something about the status and historical placing of each one and the contribution they made to theatrical work. Both editors had worked beside Shakespeare, day in and day out, through the twenty years or so of his career as a London playwright, entrepreneur, and actor, and were in a good position to know what he wrote, his working routines, the staging of his plays, and who acted in them.

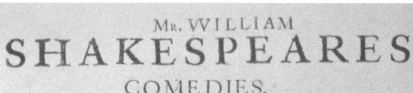

Title page of First Folio of 1623 (Shakespeare's first collected plays).

Anyone who doubts that William Shakespeare, son of a trader of Stratford-upon-Avon, was the author of the plays should look at the preliminaries of the First Folio. Its two editors were intimate with his work; they would have seen him writing and so were familiar with his handwriting. Ben Jonson, author of prefatory verses, was a fellow playwright, a contemporary, and rival. He knew Shakespeare's life and work well; he knew that as a creative writer and personality, he was, as the son of a provincial trader, glove-maker, and butcher, 'self-made'. He writes about Shakespeare's work being a success at the courts of Queen Elizabeth and King James, a period covering the whole writing life. He writes, 'even so, the race/Of Shakespeare's mind, and manners brightly shines/ In his well turned, and true filed lines.' He calls him 'Sweet Swan of Avon'— he knew of course that Shakespeare came from Stratford-upon-Avon. Can anyone seriously doubt, faced with such comments from his contemporaries, that William Shakespeare of Stratford, author and London playwright, was the author of the plays and poems attributed to him?

An intriguing fact about this volume is that in the preliminaries, a laudatory sonnet by Hugh Holland (1569–1633) appears. He was born in Denbigh, son of Robert Holland, and was buried in Westminster Abbey. That he was asked by the editors of the 'First Folio' to write about Shakespeare suggests that they knew he was acquainted with the playwright's life and work. This suggests time spent in theatrical circles in London say between 1592 and 1612. During the earlier part of this period, John Salusbury, also of Denbigh, was also intermittently in London, where he was knighted by Queen Elizabeth in 1601 for his help in quelling the Essex rebellion, and also mixing with theatre people. It is reasonable to assume that they were acquainted.

There is no mystery about the authorship. The mystery is elsewhere. Where was Shakespeare for the first third of his life? How did he manage to write so much? Why did he do it? How did he do it? What happened to his manuscripts? Who were his friends, acquaintances, and patrons?

Let us turn our attention back to the first third of his life. The 'missing years' are, say, 1578–9 (when he probably left school) to 1592 (when he was definitely in London). We have the four events previously mentioned, but nothing else to say where he was and what he was doing. How can we produce background material when we have no foreground material? Except, here we focus on a single event, a name appearing in an obscure will in the north of England: the will of Alexander Houghton. On the blank sheet of Shakespeare's early life, one ostensible mark appears in 1581, which challenges us. The will takes up four pages (Appendix A) in Honigmann's 1985 book. It is mentioned by most biographers of Shakespeare of the last twenty years. It was brought to the foreground by Ian Wilson in his *Shakespeare: The Evidence: Unlocking the Mysteries of the Man and his Work* (Headline, 1993). The name in the will is 'William Shakeshafte'. Is this William Shakespeare? If it is, the Lancashire

Theory (the theory that Shakespeare spent most of his 'missing years' in Lancashire) is likely to be correct. If it is not, the theory is likely to be incorrect. 'William Shakeshafte now dwelling with me ...' he says (literally because the will would have been dictated to a lawyer's clerk or scrivener). He was dwelling at Lea (pronounced by locals as lee-ugh), called Lea Old Hall on some maps, in a lovely position overlooking the north bank of the Ribble river, a few miles to the west of Preston. Shakespeare could well have been here. As a piece of the jigsaw, top left, it takes its place.

'William Shakeshafte' presents a formidable challenge to scholars and biographers who want certainty. They might want to believe it was 'our' Shakespeare, but they dare not for fear of losing reputation. There is no hard evidence that William Shakespeare was in Lancashire any time between 1579 and 1592. Yet, 'William Shakeshafte' comes back to haunt us. What if it is William Shakespeare? What if the Lancashire Theory is right? If we do not allow that possibility, we might miss a great deal. Let us look again at the life, at references in relevant books and documents, and ask ourselves: does some of this point in a certain direction? Does the blank of Shakespeare's early life slowly begin to turn in to a hazy but coherent picture (with many pieces still missing)?

There is a *lacuna* in most recent biographies of Shakespeare, which is embarrassing, because William Shakespeare did live through this 'lost' period; he had his being; he occupied space and time like the rest of us. He was in London in 1592 (Greene and Nashe say so, in effect). So where was he from 1578 to 1592?

In June 1940, in wartime London, Alan Keen, antiquarian bookseller, came across an old book with handwritten notes in the margin. It was Halle's *Chronicle* (1548), which Shakespeare used as his principal source for his English history plays. Did the handwriting in this book of Keen's belong to Shakespeare? More of this later.

Why did Shakespeare write sequential history plays, based on the Wars of the Roses and the Lancastrian succession, so early in his playwriting career? Not happy to have written four (the minor tetralogy), he later wrote another four (the major tetralogy), which covered largely the same ground but in a different way. It was a task of considerable difficulty, requiring much research from sources that were not always reliable. These eight history plays illustrate the Lancastrian cause and include the history of the Stanley family, not always reliably. Could the answer be that he was writing to please his employers? The Fourth and Fifth Earls of Derby (West Derby, south Lancashire, now Merseyside), for whom he was seemingly working in London in 1592 when his first public play, 1 *Henry VI*, was performed at The Rose, were his employers years earlier. His history plays were a way of bringing their family in to prominence, paying back their financial and domestic support and earning their patronage.

The poet Edmund Spenser was a contemporary of Shakespere and despite living in Ireland for much of his life, he knew the 'scene' in writer-patronage circles in England. One small but very significant comment by Spenser—indicating that Shakespeare was in the entourage of the Stanleys—has not been much noticed by commentators, and not given the attention it deserves. A later chapter devoted to Spenser will explain this.

Henry Stanley, Fourth Earl of Derby, had two 'natural' daughters, Dorothy and Ursula, from his 'second family' residing at Hawarden Castle, Flintshire. The Stanleys had extensive land holdings in north-east Wales as well as in central and southern Lancashire, around the grand houses, Lathom, near Ormskirk, and Knowsley, now in Merseyside. In 1586, Ursula married John Salusbury, squire of Lleweni, a mansion near Denbigh, north-east Wales. He was the second son of Catrin of Berain. Berain was, and is, a Tudor house with land a few miles to the west of St Asaph, Denbighshire. Shakespeare's poem, known as *The Phoenix and the Turtle* was first printed in a book (1601) dedicated to Sir John Salusbury. A later chapter offers a new interpretation of this poem. John Salusbury was infatuated by Dorothy, Ursula's sister, as proved by his many poems, originally edited and published by Parry (printed in the Carleton Brown volume) and dedicated to her. A later chapter will reveal how Shakespeare's poem 'A Lover's Complaint' fits in with the biography of John and Dorothy (who does the complaining.)

Shakespeare, it seems, had some acquaintance with John Salusbury, and I make the case that the latter could feature as one of the three noble, wealthy, attractive young men who fascinated the writer of the sonnets.

Another part of our study is the volume *Lives of the Noble Grecians and Romans*, Sir Thomas North's translation (1579) of Plutarch's original. A copy of this book, an important source of many of Shakespeare's Roman plays, is in the Shakespeare Centre, Henley Street, Stratford-upon-Avon. This volume has annotations that show that it originally belonged to Henry, the Fourth Earl of Derby (1531–93). A certain 'William' is cited in handwriting as a recipient of this volume—who was he?

In the category of influences and inspirations that went in to the writing of his plays, we can ask: are there any other plays (apart from the eight Histories) that show a Lancashire or Stanley influence? Certainly two: *Love's Labour's Lost* and *A Midsummer Night's Dream*. The former was written early, in 1591–1593, with the latter in 1594–1595. The earlier play, I believe, features guarded, discreet, sub-textual references to Ferdinando the Fifth Earl of Derby, and the second play similarly to William, his brother, the Sixth Earl, fitting the circumstances of his marriage. It is noticeable that the first four history plays and the two mentioned above were written before mid-1595—in the early years of Shakespeare's writing career, when his then possible patrons, the Earls of Derby, would have had maximum influence upon his life and writing.

A writer will naturally use the world around him. Shakespeare was born and raised in Stratford-upon-Avon. It is natural, therefore, that the life of this small but important market town is reflected in his writing—its fields, flowers, trees, brooks, houses, tradespeople, 'the middle classes', gentry, traditions, conventions, schooling, churches, goods and chattels, and so on. Yet there is more than this in his work. There are many references to water, tides, winds, sails, shores, and hills (sometimes with the sun rising behind them); also, there is knowledge of life in great country houses and a sense of western location ('my Hounds/ Uncouple in the Western Valley' says Theseus in *A Midsummer Night's Dream*: Act IV, Scene 1). These are not the settings of workaday life in Stratford or the topography of Warwickshire. This is imagery and location of a different kind, and if Shakespeare did spend time in Lancashire, beginning with a sojourn on the banks of the Ribble, proceeding to living in the grand houses of the Derbys, this would be expected imagery.

So, I have come to the point where all the principal relevant material on my theme—Shakespeare's missing years—needs to be presented in detail. This introduction has touched on some of the reasons why the Lancashire Theory should be taken seriously. The following chapters will enable the reader to consider the matter fully, so that the theory can be examined and evaluated.

1

The Stanley Dynasty and Playing

*It is common sense to suppose that Shakespeare had won his spurs as a player
and a dramatist before being allowed to re-shape work by so famous a writer
as Greene, and this implies a period of apprenticeship previous to 1592. In
what company or companies he served is unknown, but most authorities
believe that in 1592 he was working for Lord Strange's Men who had lately
beaten the Queen's men out of the field both at court and in popular favour ...*

J. Dover Wilson, *The Essential Shakespeare*, p. 47

The Earls of Derby were and are one of the major families of Britain. Their
present title goes back to 27 October 1485, conferred by Henry Tudor (Henry
VII) upon Thomas, Lord Stanley, for his help in securing Henry's victory over
Richard III at Bosworth, near Leicester, some two months earlier. Thomas's
younger brother, William, also fought at Bosworth, allegedly rescuing Henry
Tudor at a critical moment, striking down the king and rescuing his crown
from a thorn bush, then handing it to his brother who placed it on Henry's
head. This tale, almost certainly apocryphal, smacks of Tudor myth-making
or, in current terms, spin-doctoring. Henry made William Knight of the Garter
and granted him additional lands, which made him the richest commoner in
England. However, things went badly wrong between them and Sir William
Stanley was executed on 16 February 1495.

Earlier, the title Earl of Derby was taken by Edward III's son, John of Gaunt,
who had married Henry's daughter Blanche. John of Gaunt's son Henry
Bolingbroke succeeded to the throne as Henry IV in 1399.

In Baines's *History of Lancashire*, the following appears:

A notable tradition yet remaining in the noble family of Stanley is that when
Henry VII, after the execution of Sir William Stanley, brother of Thomas, Earl
of Derby, came to progress into these parts he was entertained by the Earl at

his house at Lathom, and after a view of the whole house he was conducted by His Lordship to the top of the leads for a prospect of the country. The Earl's Fool was in company, who, observing the King draw near to the edge of the leads, not guarded with bannisters, stepped up to the Earl, and pointing down the precipice said 'Tom, remember Will.' The King understood the meaning and made haste down stairs and out of the house, and the Fool long after seemed mightily concerned that his Lord had not courage to take that opportunity of avenging himself for the death of his brother.

Before Bosworth, Thomas, Second Lord Stanley, had married, secondly, Margaret, daughter and heiress of John, Duke of Somerset. She was the widow of Edmund Tudor, Earl of Richmond, and mother of Henry, Earl of Richmond. This Henry, the first Tudor king, Henry VII, awarded his step-father the title of Lord High Steward of England on the day of his coronation in March 1486.

The armorial bearings of the Stanleys, originated with William de Stanley in 1316, are 'Arg, on a bend asure, three Stags Head, cabossed, Or'. William acquired the hereditary office of Master Forester of Wirral; this was mentioned in 1306 and 1307. In 1405, Sir John Stanley was awarded a grant of the Isle of Man, which the family ruled until 1736. He was Treasurer of the Royal Household and Lord of the Isle of Man.

Our narrative starts with Henry Stanley, Fourth Earl of Derby. He was born in September 1531, summoned to Parliament for 1559–1576, admitted to Gray's Inn on 24 January 1562, and graduated with an MA from Oxford on 6 September 1566. He succeeded his father in 1572 as Lord Lieutenant of Lancaster and Chester, an office he held until his death. In October 1586, he was one of the commissioners for the trial of Mary, Queen of Scots; this comprised twenty-four noblemen, including nine earls.

He married Margaret, the first daughter of Henry (Clifford) and Eleanor, on 7 February 1555, in the Royal Chapel, Whitehall. Eleanor was the first daughter of Mary (Tudor), eldest daughter of Henry VII. So, Henry Stanley married in to Tudor blood. His children from Margaret had Henry of Richmond, Henry VII of England, as their great-great-grandfather.

Henry's wife, Margaret, (says *Burke's Peerage*) was looked upon (*c.* 1557) by many Englishmen as the legal heir presumptive of the crown. On this account, she was an object of suspicion to the Queen, and in May 1580, she was under restraint. Camden says that she had 'a womanish curiosity' in prying into the future, 'consulting with wizards'.

Henry, Fourth Earl of Derby, died at Lathom, 25 September 1593 and was buried 4 December 1593, at Ormskirk, aged sixty-two.

Henry had four sons by his marriage to Margaret (Clifford): William, who died young; Ferdinando, born 1560, matriculated Oxford in 1572 (becoming the Fifth Earl); William, born 1561, matriculated Oxford in 1572 (becoming the Sixth Earl); Francis, born 1562, matriculated Oxford in 1572. So, there were three boys born in successive years being admitted formally to membership of the University of Oxford from St John's College in the same year (aged ten, eleven, and twelve—it seems inconceivably young from our perspective).

Henry had a 'second family'. When living at his castle at Hawarden, he lived with Jane Halsall and by her had four children, 'natural' but acknowledged. The eldest was Dorothy; by December 1588, she was married to Sir Cuthbert Halsall, a distant relative. The second daughter, Ursula, married John Salusbury of Denbigh in 1586. The third child, Thomas, became Thomas Stanley of Eccleshall with an estate in Kirkby, Lancashire. The fourth child, Henry, had an estate in Ormskirk. During October 1588 at New Park, one of the Stanley residences, close to Lathom, it was noted by Farington, the household steward 'mr henry stanley junior came & went.'

Henry's son Ferdinando, who features strongly in our story, married Alice Spencer, daughter of Sir John Spencer of Althorp (an ancestor of the deceased Diana, Princess of Wales) in or shortly before 1580. They had three children, all girls—Anne (b. 1580), Frances (b. 1583), and Elizabeth (b. 1588). Anne (who features in our narrative) married Grey Brydges (Fifth Baron Chandos of Sudeley) on 28 February 1607 or 1608 and, secondly, the Second Earl of Castlehaven in 1624. She was buried on 11 October 1647 at Harefield.

An interesting entry from a family tree of the Stanleys reads as follows:

FERDINANDO, 5th Earl. This nobleman having been tampered with by one Hesketh, to assume the title of king in right of his grandmother, and rejecting the proposition indignantly, is supposed to have been poisoned in consequence by the conspirators. His death occurred 16 April, 1594, when the baronies of Stanley and Strange fell into abeyance amongst his three daughters, and the earldom devolved upon his brother ... WILLIAM, succeeded his brother as the 6th Earl, K.G. This nobleman bought from his nieces their claim on the Isle of Man; married 26 June, 1594, and died in 1642.

An alternative version is that members of Queen Elizabeth's retainers had Ferdinando poisoned because he could have claimed the crown after her.

The claim that William the Sixth Earl of Derby married Elizabeth, eldest daughter of Edward Vere, Seventeenth Earl of Oxford, in June 1594 (repeated in the pedigree books) is false. The wedding might have been planned for this date but in fact, it took place in January 1595. The reason for the delay is said to be dowager Alice's pregnancy. Had she given birth to a boy, he would have inherited the earldom and William would have been 'un-earled'. She apparently miscarried (or the pregnancy was a falsity) and the wedding went ahead in London, to great ceremony, attended by Queen Elizabeth.

Ian Wilson, in his interesting book *Shakespeare: The Evidence*, writes:

> Protestant historians have almost invariably dismissed Ferdinando's poisoning as straightforward Catholic vengeance for Hesketh's execution, but this was certainly not how Ferdinando's continental-based cousin Sir William Stanley and his fellow Catholic exiles saw it in 1594: 'Yorke said, 'It is no marvel, when Machiavellian policies govern England. I durst pawn my life that the Lord Treasurer [i.e. Lord Burghley] caused him to be poisoned that he [Ferdinando] being dead he [Burghley] might marry the young Lady Vere unto the brother of the said Earl of Derby.'
>
> ... Burghley had everything to fear from a convincingly kingly great lord who at any time of weakness, such as upon Elizabeth's death, might well be swept to the throne by Catholics as a perfectly legitimate successor to Elizabeth, thus ruining all the Protestant policies Burghley had so long pursued as Elizabeth's first minister. With Ferdinando dead, on the other hand, and the unmarried and easily manipulable [*sic*] 'nidicock' William in his place, a marriage of Burleigh's granddaughter with this William would propel her straight into the power seat of the Stanley-Derby empire, thus enabling the sort of defusion [*sic*] of opposition that all his life Burghley had built his reputation upon.

This 'defusion [*sic*] of opposition' includes the capital punishment of Mary Queen of Scots, and of Thomas Salusbury of Denbigh, John Salusbury's elder brother (another of Tudor blood, through their mother Catrin of Berain), because of his part in the Babington Plot to kill Queen Elizabeth in 1586.

A letter written a fortnight or so after her husband's death, from Lathom, by Alice, Countess of Derby, to Sir Robert Cecil, is worth quoting in full for its style and opinion:

> I must entreat the continuance of your kind favours towards me in a cause wherein I have written to the Lords and others of the Privy Council, and for that it will come to your view, I must desire you to effect what I have entreated their Honours unto, the matter being so just as you shall find it is, and I hope my lord your father's wonted favour will not be drawn from me by any means or persuasions, albeit I hear of a motion of marriage between the Earl, my brother, and my lady Vere, your niece, but how true the news is I know not, only I wish her a better husband.

If this marriage was the one Shakespeare wrote *A Midsummer Night's Dream* for, then May 1594 could be the real time that lies behind the 'rite of May' allusion of the play (and other springtime allusions). Shakespeare was in all probability penning this play in the winter of 1593 and the spring of 1594 (scholars generally agree that it was written at this time, with revisions later in the year) when the marriage was expected in June (Midsummer) but it was, as we said, postponed—due to Alice's pregnancy or alleged pregnancy—until the following January. As a writer for the Derbys, a commission to write a wedding play for the family would be entirely expected.

Lathom House and Knowsley were the two main Stanley houses in Lancashire, with another, New Park, close to Lathom. All three residences housed the family and entertaining occurred in each, with an emphasis on Lathom, which was the largest and where retainers, servants, teachers, and players were put up. Lathom was built in the form of a fortified castle, having a string of towers in the outer wall, two inner courtyards, and the central Eagle Tower.

There is no doubt that the Stanleys lived in great style. A. L. Rowse, in his fine book *The England of Elizabeth* writes:

> When the Earl of Derby went on embassy to France in 1584 he had a train of 130 gentlemen in two liveries, one of purple and gold lace, one of black satin and taffeta, all with their gold chains ... This same Earl of Derby, when residing quietly in the country at Lathom in 1587, had a household of 118 servants ... The Derby household was presided over by 3 officers, steward, comptroller and receiver general, each with 3 servants, while my lord had 7 gentlemen in waiting and a page. In 1590 the household had increased to 140 servants for a family of five. (pp. 253–254)

An informative booklet published by the Lathom Park Trust in 2005 declares:

> It was in 1385 that Lathom passed into the Stanley family, with the marriage of Isabel de Lathom to Sir John Stanley, whose family already owned large tracts of North-West England. Under the Stanleys, Lathom grew to become the principal regional seat of power for almost 300 years, and in effect became the 'Northern Court' of Tudor and Stuart England ... By the end of the 16th century, the Stanley family held the title of the Earls of Derby, the Lords of Man and the Lord-Lieutenants of Lancashire, and they were the virtual feudal overlords of the Hundred of West Derby. (pp. 8–9)

The period 1586–9 is covered by the Derby Household Books; we are very fortunate that these have survived and have appeared in print. William Farington (1537–1610) was their author. His notes of callers to the Stanley houses and events inside are brief, incomplete, but very interesting. An essay titled 'A Model for Malvolio' by Beatrice Lilley makes a case for Farington being the 'original' for Malvolio, and also Oswald (from *King Lear*). Many play-groups are noted as visiting the houses, including those of Sir Thomas

Hesketh at Christmas 1587. John Salusbury of Denbigh was a frequent visitor, with his wife Ursula (Earl Henry's 'natural' daughter). In August 1587, 'On Sonday a greate company,' and a list of foodstuffs is appended for an occasion of feasting and entertainment. In 1589, the close relationship between the Stanleys and the Heskeths is shown in the remark, 'Thursdaie my L. & Lady Strange went to dinner at Rufford.' Rufford was the Hesketh's home. Also in 1589, '& the same daye came Mr Salebury & his unkell & dyvers others.'

In the summer and autumn of 1587, Earl Henry arranged a festival of plays at Lathom. Henry had his own troupe of players, 'Derby's Men', who had attracted audiences in Coventry, Exeter, Dover, and Stratford-upon-Avon. They played at court in 1580. As well as his own players, visiting troupes to Lathom and Knowsley between May 1587 and August 1590 included the Queens Players, the Earl of Essex's Players, Sir Thomas Hesketh's Players, the Earl of Leicester's Players, and three unnamed groups.

Henry's son Ferdinando was involved in plays and playing. As early as 1579–80, when he was twenty-one, 'Lord Strange's Tumblers' were entertaining at court. They toured the country and for four years, they entertained the Queen at Christmas festivities: 'sundry feates of Tumbling and activity were shown before her Majestie on New years day at night by Lord Strange his servants.' When the Earl of Leicester died on 4 September 1588, Lord Strange's group (which seem by this time to have merged with his father's troupe) combined with experienced actors from Leicester's disbanded company. These included Augustine Phillips, Thomas Pope, Richard Burbage, George Bryan, William Kemp, John Heminge, Henry Condell, William Sly, John Duke, Christopher Beeston, and Alexander Cooke. A great playing group was born. This is possibly where, when, and why Shakespeare's serious playwriting began. The new troupe needed plays to perform and he started writing them. Eric Sams has studied the plays *Edmund Ironside* and *Edward III* in exhaustive detail and pronounced them Shakespeare's early work, dating between 1587 and 1589. We should note here that historically, Edward III was the father of John of Gaunt and thus founded the Lancastrian royal dynasty.

Michael Wood, in his book *In Search of Shakespeare*, writes:

> Shakespeare's primary relationships in the theatre through his entire professional life were with the Burbage family: James, the entrepreneur responsible for the first custom-built public theatre in the modern world in 1576; his sons Cuthbert, later manager of the Globe, and Richard, the great actor. So how and where did they meet? Their earlier connection has never been discovered, but it could go back to Warwickshire. James Burbage is first found with Robert Dudley's players in Warwick ... (p. 108)

This 'early connection' may well have taken place when, following Dudley, the Earl of Leicester's death in September 1588, his playing troupe, including

Richard Burbage (*c.* 1568–1619) joined with Lord Strange's. He certainly was a member of Strange's as reorganised under the Lord Chamberlain's patronage in 1594. In Shakespeare's will, his friend ('ffelowe') Burbage is left 28*s* 8*d* to buy a ring.

In 1589, the newly assembled playing group of Henry and Ferdinando were playing at the Cross Keys Inn in Gracechurch Street, London. At Christmas 1591–2, they were entertaining at court. E. K. Chambers, in his *William Shakespeare A Study of Facts and Problems*, p. 307, records the following: '1591–2. Court (Whitehall). Dec. 27, 28; Jan. 1, 9; Feb. 6, 8. Ye seruantes of ye lo: Straunge ... for six severall playes.'

The last remark probably indicates six performances of more than one play. Given the arrangement of the three pairs of performances, might it not be possible that the three parts of Shakespeare's new history play, *Henry VI* was first performed here at Whitehall (the present site of the Houses of Lords and Commons) starting on 27 December 1591?

From February to June 1592, Ferdinando, Lord Strange's, players were the resident company at the Rose, the playhouse that Philip Henslowe had recently restored on the Bankside. Anthony Burgess writes:

> The Rose, rethatched, replastered, repainted, refurbished at a total cost of £100, was ready in February, 1592, to house Lord Strange's Men. This was a distinguished company ... and it was led by the most accomplished actor of the day—Edward Alleyn. On February 19 the troupe opened a busy season with a comedy by Robert Greene ... But on February 26, a Saturday, there was a packed house for a play by Christopher Marlowe—*The Jew of Malta*. On the following Friday, March 3, a chronicle play was presented which drew the highest takings of the entire season. It was called *Henry VI* and we know, though the audience did not, that its author was William Shakespeare.

> Anthony Burgess, *Shakespeare*, p. 98

Burgess continues: 'Shakespeare had joined the best acting company of the day at some time between 1587 and 1592. He had left the Queen's men, if he had ever belonged to the Queen's Men, along with Will Kemp, who was now chief clown at Lord Strange's.' (p. 98).

Peter Ackroyd, that outstanding contemporary writer on English culture and history, writes the following on page 224 of *Albion*:

> The early sequence of the history plays represents the first serious and prolonged attempt to introduce the English chronicles to the stage; in a nation (or city) obsessed with its past, they proved instantly popular. Shakespeare had devined the native mood, and expressed a genuine native spirit, in dramas

which reflect the bloodthirstiness and disparagement of death commonly associated with the English. They are in part designed to legitimise the dynasty of the Tudors, and thus bring a political interpretation to bear upon English history, but they are also filled with an egalitarian spirit in the exploits of Pistol and Mistress Quickly.

When the new patron's father, the Fourth Earl of Derby, died on 25 September 1593, the company again changed its title, to that of 'The Earl of Derby's Servants'. The new Earl, Ferdinando, lived less than seven months longer, almost certainly poisoned, dying on 16 April 1594. For a short period after that, the group called itself 'The Countess of Derby's Players'.

In June 1594, an influential, constant, London-based patron took over this talented playing group. He was Henry Carey, First Lord Hunsdon, who held (from 1585) the office of Lord Chamberlain. According to extant lists of the two companies, the following actors passed in 1594 from the service of the Earl of Derby, (formerly Lord Strange), deceased, to that of the Lord Chamberlain (Lord Hunsdon): Richard Burbadge, William Kemp, Thomas Pope, John Heminges, Augustine Phillips, George Bryan, Harry Condell, Will Sly, Richard Cowley, John Duke, and Christopher Beeston. These lists, drawn from workaday theatricals, do not include William Shakespeare; the explanation could be that he was busy writing plays (and poems) rather than playing. Here we have the playing group that in 1594 was called 'The Chamberlain's Men', with William Shakespeare as their principal playwriter and part shareholder.

2

Stratford-upon-Avon, Schooling, and Leaving

So there was no sheltered upbringing for young Shakespeare. Through his father's wheeler-dealing the child was brought into contact with every level of society, with the world of business and of profit and loss, and it would come out later in his language. As a mature writer he would be particularly good at social interaction, especially between men. Even the gaps in colloquial speech, the things left out, are very precisely observed.

Michael Wood, *In Search of Shakespeare*, p. 43

All the elements of Shakespeare's life seem to come together within his drama. The folk-tales of his Warwickshire childhood and his schoolboy reading of Latin literature, for example, combine in his creation of classical enchantments. But his biography provides other conclusions. The 'missing years', when he may have been a tutor in a recusant household, contain the mystery without which no life of a writer is complete. His journey to London and his employment as an actor prepared him for the hard and raucous business of the stage. His early success as a dramatist, far eclipsing any success as an actor, directly resulted in his ability to please the crowd. But even though he never stopped writing for that many-headed hydra, he had aspirations towards gentility and coveted his own coat-of-arms; he was also a successful businessman, who owned property in both London and Stratford. He can never be fully identified with either place, and his hovering between two worlds seems wholly appropriate in a man of such equivocal personality.

Peter Ackroyd, *Albion*, p. 220

It is not necessary to detail the well-known Stratford background; a few main biographical points will suffice. William Shakespeare, the writer of the plays of the First Folio, was undoubtedly born in this town in April 1564. His father was John Shakespeare (*c.* 1529–1601); his mother was Mary (Arden) (*c.* 1540–1608).

They had eight children: four girls and four boys. The first two children, girls, died young; then came William (1563–1616), their first son. The other children were Gilbert (1566–1612), Joan (1569–1646), Ann (1571–1579), Richard (1574–1613), and Edmund (1580–1607). Edmund became an actor in London; little is known of him except that he was buried at St Saviour's, Southwark, on 31 December 1607. He is not seen as having any professional association there with his famous brother.

Famously, we do not know the day when William was born. We only know (and thank goodness for this fact) that he was christened at the fifteenth-century font of Holy Trinity Church, Stratford-upon-Avon, on 26 April 1564. The parish register of Holy Trinity records this baptism but also that of seven younger brothers and sisters. The original entry document is in safe keeping at the Birthplace Trust, Henley Street.

Shakespeare was buried in the chancel of Holy Trinity Church in 1616. This privilege was bestowed upon him as a 'lay rector', which he became in 1605. Alongside his grave are those of his widow Anne and other members of his family. Nearby on the north wall is a bust of William, the original of which was erected within seven years of his death and in the lifetime of his widow and many of his friends. The image on this memorial has given rise to many observations. However, let us remind ourselves of what John Aubrey wrote about him: 'a handsome well shap'd man: very good company, and of a redie and pleasant wit.' William Beeston, a playing colleague of Shakespeare's, noted: 'he was not a company keeper' and that he 'wouldn't be debauched and if invited to, writ, he was in paine.' This comment illustrates his fastidious way of life and judicious use of his time. He was exceptionally hard-working.

If he was unable to properly handwrite his complete name on each page of his will of 1616, its cause was likely to be his final illness combined with overwork, especially by the right hand and arm (see Ian Wilson's discussion of 'scriver's palsy' or 'writer's cramp' on pages 385–386 of *Shakespeare: The Evidence*). However, his inscription 'By me William Shakespeare' on the final page (the first to be inscribed) seems to state that the will was handwritten by himself. However, this seems unlikely; it was most likely penned by a lawyer's clerk. Sir Sidney Lee, on page 142 of his 1916 biography, refers to 'Shakespeare, with his gigantic powers of work'. He handwrote over thirty-six plays, roughly two a year, and two long narrative poems. Unfortunately, not a single undisputed sheet of this huge output has survived. However, the anonymous Tudor manuscript play *Edmund Ironside* (fifth in the British Library collection Egerton 1994) was both handwritten and composed by Shakespeare, according to Eric Sams. Also, many authorities say that 'Hand D', a section of the handwritten manuscript of the play *Sir Thomas More* was also composed and handwritten by Shakespeare.

William Shakespeare grew up in Stratford. He was lucky to survive. When he was three months old, the plague hit the town and one in seven of its inhabitants died. Later, in London, especially in the years 1592–1593 and 1603, he was to witness the plague, but again he survived (helped, no doubt, by his departure with travelling players, stays in Stratford—perhaps twice in a year—and accommodation by patrons and employers in their country estates).

In Stratford, his father contributed to the relief of the destitute. On 4 July 1565, John Shakespeare was elected Alderman and from 1567, he was accorded the prefix 'Mr', meaning 'Master', 'a title which men give to esquires and other gentlemen.' In his book, *The Real Shakespeare*, Eric Sams encapsulates the trades of John Shakespeare in to one sentence: 'butcher, whitawer, and his description as "agricola", tenant farmer, substantial land-owner, or "yeoman", all fit together, like his work as a glover, wool-dealer, and moneylender over many years.' (p. 9) The Queen's Company of players and the Earl of Worcester's Company each received from John Shakespeare an official welcome, and gave a performance in the Guildhall before the council: his encouragement of playing proved that he was no puritan. In 1575, he purchased two houses in Stratford; one of them (the traditional 'birthplace' in Henley Street) adjoined the tenement acquired nineteen years before.

However, in 1578, he was unable to pay the weekly sum of four pence for the relief of the poor, or his contribution 'towards the furniture of three pikemen, two billmen, and one archer'. On 12 November 1578, John and Mary Shakespeare and George Gibbes transferred seventy acres of land for cash. On 19 November 1578, John Shakespeare is exempted from paying a weekly tax for the poor, levied on aldermen. Throughout 1578, John Shakespeare is absent from all eight recorded meetings of the Stratford council.

With five children at home, the finances of the Shakespeare family were overstretched. To meet his growing liabilities, the father borrowed money from his wife's kinsfolk, and he and his wife mortgaged Asbies, her valuable property at Wilmcote, for £40 during Easter Term, 1579. The following year, Mary's share of her late father's property and land in Snittersfield was sold by John and Mary. John was called 'yeoman' and both signed with marks.

John Shakespeare, as an alderman, was entitled to free education for his four sons. A large expansion of grammar schooling in Henry VII's reign brought Stratford Grammar School into being. It was refashioned by Edward VI in 1553. William Shakespeare probably joined the school in 1571 when Walter Roche BA, schoolmaster, was retiring in favour of Simon Hunt BA. Hunt left in 1575 for the Catholic seminary in Douai; he later became a Jesuit in Rome. In 1575, Thomas Jenkins took over the school and in 1579, John Cottom. Roche had held a Lancashire fellowship at his college, Corpus Christi. Hunt and Cottom were also Oxford graduates.

Nicholas Rowe (1674–1718), the first critical editor of Shakespeare and author of a short *Life* wrote:

[His father] had bred him, 'tis true , for some time at a Free-school, where 'tis probable he acquir'd that little Latin he was master of; but the narrowness of his circumstances, and the want of his assistance at home, forc'd his father to withdraw him from thence, and unhappily prevented his further proficiency in that Language.

Latin was the language of instruction in school, so this comment, which has a ring of authenticity, points to his leaving school before the usual time; Sams suggests this happened when aged thirteen.

William Shakespeare turned thirteen in April 1577. 'I have been told heretofore,' wrote the diarist Aubrey, 'by some of the neighbours that when he was a boy he exercised his father's trade.' Rowe, in 1709, also said: 'Upon his leaving School, he seems to have given entirely into that way of Living which his Father propos'd to him.'

If he left school in the summer of 1577 (or when he was fourteen in 1578) to help his father, that gave him time to experience the trades and natural life of rural England, which are so plentiful in his writing. The loss of his mother's family property, Asbies (he would have been proud of her lineage, from the landed family of Ardens), in 1579 and the sale of her inheritance at Snittersfield in 1580 would have had a depressing effect upon him. His sister Ann died, aged seven, in April 1579. His younger siblings Gilbert, Richard, Edmund, and Joan were, in all likelihood, living at home. If he left Stratford for Lancashire, this would be about the time. Things were bad at home; he had no prospects. He needed to make his way in the world. On 11 February 1579, Lord Strange's men were paid for a theatrical performance at Stratford. He may not have seen their performance, but he is likely to have seen the players about the streets, in their livery of silver and blue (azure), displaying the eagle motif of the Stanleys. They could be seen as representing a grand life, of glamour, order and good income, contrasting with his impoverished no-hope state in Stratford. It is tempting to think that he may have joined them at this significant point in time, but there is very little evidence for recruitment by travelling players in the Elizabethan period.

He was tainted by his father's Catholicism; John Shakespeare's name appeared, later, on a list of recusants (those who did not regularly attend Protestant church services). The players in the Stratford streets were from Lancashire. John Cottom, schoolmaster, was a Lancashire man; he could have made the introductions and the travel arrangements. Once a County Palatine, with powers resembling that of the Sovereign, its chief nobleman was Henry, the Fourth Earl of Derby, Lord Strange's father. In Lancashire, protected by wealthy Catholic families, the young William would be safe; he would have decent accommodation and he could earn a living.

He married a local woman at the end of 1582, when he was only eighteen-and-a-half and she twenty-six. However, if he left school in 1577–8 and stayed in Stratford, is it likely that he—a boy of exceptional intelligence and ability in writing (creatively and orthographically)—spent four or five years of perhaps the most vivid years of his life living with his parents in Stratford and working at his father's humdrum businesses? I think it is very unlikely. I think his ambition will have kicked in and an entire change in direction has to be considered. He might well have gone to Lancashire.

A. L. Rowse's *The England of Elizabeth* carries a chapter 'Catholics and Puritans'. The following is quoted from pages 446–451:

> Catholic Recusancy became an intractable problem. Its [the government's] worst failure was in Lancashire, the only English county where Catholicism survived continuously on any scale. This 'so unbridled and bad an handful of England'—as Lord Strange, Derby's eldest son, called it—gave the government any amount of trouble ... West and North Lancashire were under the domination of their gentry, who remained conservative and Catholic ... The situation in Lancashire did not improve for all the government's efforts: in 1590 there were some 700 Recusants presented (in Cheshire 200): there was nothing like such a proportion anywhere else. Bishop Chadderton had a supporter in Earl Derby's son and heir, Lord Strange, between whom and his father there was a certain tension: 'To be constant is no common virtue,' wrote his son, 'although it be most commendable, most fit and least found in noblemen.' It seems that they both thought that the Earl's temporising policy was responsible for the ill-success of the campaign in Lancashire ... A Stanley, he continued the family tradition of being on both sides. In Derby hundred as late as 1590, out of seventy-one names among the gentry, only ten were reliable supporters of the reformed religion.... Catholicism survived on a geographical basis: in Lancashire notably in three areas—in Ribblesdale about Stonyhurst, in the Fylde country and along the fertile coastal area from Liverpool to Southport ...

Rowse goes on to comment:

> It was quite common for Lancashire families to have a Recusant schoolmaster, who was sometimes a priest, in the house: Mrs Houghton of the Lea kept one of the Blundells as such, who taught her children to sing and play upon the virginals. (p.450)

There is no doubt that William Shakespeare's father, John, was a Catholic, but of course he kept it to himself. In March 1592 he was listed as a recusant, i.e. one who 'refused obstinately to resort to the church' with eight other names, annotated: 'Wee suspect theese nyne persons next ensuing absent themselves for feare of process' (Sams, p. 215). On 25 September 1592, the Privy Council commissioners, headed by Sir Thomas Lucy of Stratford, again name the same nine recusants, including John Shakespeare, with the annotation: 'it is said that these last nine coom not to Churche for feare of process for debte'.

John Shakespeare made a Catholic will. Park Honan gives an excellent account:

> Did a Jesuit missionary in the 1580s persuade him to declare his faith? A paper booklet of six leaves stitched together, found by a bricklayer in April 1757 between the rafters and tiling of what had been John's western house at Henley Street, has turned out to be an authentic formulary; a 'John Shakspear' here makes a Catholic profession of faith, and appears to sign, as the last paragraph indicates, in his own hand. [This handwritten document has been lost]. The formulary found in the rafters follows Borromeo's Last Will of the Soul, which Jesuit missionaries in England were making use of by 1581. (pp. 38–39)

Some have doubted this story but Sams (p. 204, *The Real Shakespeare*), Honan and Ian Wilson (who reproduces it as Appendix C in his biography) believe the John Shakespeare will is genuine. It reads, in part (taken from Sams's uncorrected version):

> In the name of God, the father, sonne and holy ghost, the most holy and blessed Virgin Mary, mother of God, and holy host of archangels, angels, patriarchs, prophets, evangelists, apostles, saints, martyrs, and all the ecclesiastical court and company of heaven, I John Shakespear, an unworthy member of the holy Catholick religion ... I, John Shakespear do protest, that I am willing, yea, I doe infinitely desire and humbly crave, that of this my last will and testament the glorious and ever Virgin mary, mother of god, refuge and advocate of sinners (whom I honour specially above all saints) may be the chief Executresse, togeather with these other saints, my patrons, (saint Winefride) all whome I invocke and beseech to be present at the hour of my death, that she and they may comfort me with their desired presence ...

John here names Saint Winifred as his patron saint. There is only one Saint Winifred in Britain, located in Holywell, north-east Wales. Her shrine was and is a bath fed by water from a well and has for centuries been a place of pilgrimage for Catholic believers. Why should John Shakespeare in distant Stratford have this saint as his patron? There is a possible explanation: that his son visited this place (which is close to the Stanley holdings), told his father the story of Winifred and of the healing well, and his father incorporated Saint Winifred in his (very private) Catholic will.

The original version of this will was pre-printed, with spaces where individual details were to be handwritten in. These were being distributed surreptitiously in England by Thomas Campion. John Shakespeare could not handwrite. His son was an expert scribe. It is possible that William completed the document for his father, filling in the blank spaces with pertinent detail, one of which was Saint Winifred. He could have got the original printed formulary from Campion or one of his retinue, for we know that they visited the Catholic home of the Houghtons in northern Lancashire, with the young man 'Shakeshaft' in the household. (see Rowse, p. 447). Wilson notes the date of the will as '1580 [?]' although it could have been created for John Shakespeare any time before his death in 1601.

St Winifred's well, at Holywell, Flintshire, has a Derby connection: Margaret Beaufort paid for the church building which sits over the well. It is located about half-way between Denbigh, the home of John Salusbury, and Knowsley, the Derby house, then in Lancashire, a few hours' horse-ride from each.

Biographies of William Shakespeare are fond of quoting Aubrey's remark, 'for he had been in his younger years a Schoolmaster in the Countrey.' This comment came from William Beeston, whose father Christopher Beeston had been a player-colleague of Shakespeare's (and, noted Honan, had acted with him in Ben Jonson's *Every Man in his Humour*). It carries conviction. 'In the country' precludes London and Stratford and any urban place. Rural Lancashire would be 'in the country' and A. L. Rowse's discovery of a 'schoolmaster' employed by the Hoghtons of Lea, on the Ribble, Lancashire, chimes with the details of the will of Lea's Alexander Hoghton of 1581, with its high opinion of two young men of his household, one of which was 'Shakeshafte'. Beeston would have known some of the close personal details of the players employed in the Derby household through his father. This adds weight to the supposition that the young William Shakespeare was a private tutor employed in the Hoghton and, later, Stanley households. Sams confirms that the term 'schoolmaster' applied, at the time, to a private tutor.

The biographical expert in this area is Professor Ernst Honigmann. In his introduction to *Shakespeare: The 'Lost Years'*, he poses the pertinent question:

How does a gifted youth from provincial Stratford, without a university background or degree, find employment as a schoolmaster? The obvious answer is that he must have been recommended as capable of the work of a schoolmaster, or an assistant master, even though he had no degree. Anyone in Stratford could have recommended him, but one person in particular would have been an invaluable referee: the schoolmaster at Stratford's grammar school, who would be able to give an expert opinion of young Shakespeare's scholarly attainments ... when we follow up the clues we are stopped short by a remarkable coincidence ... Thomas Jenkins was succeeded in 1579 by

John Cottom ... [who] was a native of Lancashire who returned *c.* 1582 to
Tarnacre, where his family owned property ... [and this] is only ten miles
from Lea, where the Hoghtons lived.

The Hoghtons could have taken the talented, recommended, young man to
their household to teach the children of their retainers.

'Cottom,' writes Park Honan, 'was a son of Lawrence Cottam, whose
ancestral estate was at Dilworth in Lancashire; adjacent to Cottam's estate was
Alston, a country seat of Alexander de Houghton.'

Cottom's brother Thomas Cottam studied at the Jesuit college in Rome in
1579. The following year he was captured returning from Rheims with personal
effects symbolising Catholicism. He was tried, then executed at Tyburn on 30
May 1582.

Park Honan writes:

> But since there is a good possibility that he went to Hoghton, we may suppose
> that he had experiences not wholly unlike those a grammar-school boy would
> have had at Hoghton Tower and Lea, and that in 1579 or 1580, after what
> may have been a rough journey, a 'William Shakeshafte' found himself in the
> employ of a great family in the north. (p. 65)

Honan continues:

> Exactly who drew him from Stratford, or when at last he left, we do not
> know.... What is quite certain is that an expansion of playing companies in
> the 1580s would have worked in his favour. New hands were needed for all
> varieties of work in connection with the popular public entertainments; and,
> again, the capricious Ferdinando, Lord Strange, was patron of a troupe of
> acrobats and players in a position to expand. (p. 91)

Scholars such as Honigmann and Honan have subscribed to the Shakespeare/
Shakeshafte theory, along with historian Ian Wilson and writer Anthony
Holden. The magisterial E. K. Chambers has also written of it in detail in
Shakespearean Gleanings (1944). He says:

> The linking with Sir Thomas Hesketh seems to make it at least highly probable
> that Foke Gyllome and William Shakeshafte were players ... (and) it is clear
> that, if William Shakeshafte passed from the service of Alexander Houghton
> or Sir Thomas Hesketh, he might very easily have gone on into that of Lord
> Strange, and so later into the London theatrical world, where we find in 1592
> William Shakespeare ... called by the envious Robert Greene 'the only Shake-
> scene in a countrey'. (p. 56)

3

Lea, 'Shakeshafte', the Hoghtons and Heskeths

If, for example, he received his education as a singing-boy in the service of some great Catholic nobleman, it would help to explain how he became an actor, since the transition from singing-boy to stage-player was almost as inevitable at that period as the breaking of the male voice in adolescence.

J. Dover Wilson, *The Essential Shakespeare*, p. 41

We have postulated that the young William Shakespeare left Stratford-upon-Avon in 1578 or 1579, when he was fourteen or fifteen, for the north-west of Lancashire, and that he was there in the employ of Alexander Hoghton of Lea Hall for approximately two years.

The family used both Hoghton Tower and Lea Hall (now a farm called Lea Old Hall). The Right Worshipful Thomas Hoghton rebuilt Hoghton Tower between 1560 and 1565. He was born in 1518: only living five years in the rebuilt tower, Thomas, at the time of the 'Rising of the Northern Earls' (1569) went into voluntary exile, living in Lier, Antwerp. He died in Liege in 1580; ten years later, he was re-buried in the college chapel of Douai, which his close friend William Allen, now cardinal, had founded.

During those eleven years of exile, Thomas's brother, Richard Hoghton of Park Hall, Charnock, looked after his affairs and properties and twice was allowed by the government to visit his older brother abroad. Alexander Hoghton, another brother of Thomas Hoghton, continued to live between Hoghton Tower and Lea Hall during this period, where he developed his interest in the Arts, especially theatre. Alexander came in to his substantial inheritance late in life; this consisted of over 40,000 acres including various Lancashire manors. In 1580, Alexander succeeded his elder brother, Thomas.

The will of Alexander Hoghton of Lea was written on 3 August 1581 and proved on 12 September 1581. Alexander had his own players and minstrels. The part we are interested in reads as follows:

Item; it is my mind & will that the said Thomas Hoghton of 'brynescoules' my brother shall have all my instruments belonging to musics, & all manner of play clothes if he be minded to keep & do keep players. And if he will not keep & maintain players, then it is my mind and will that Sir Thomas Hesketh knight shall have the same instruments & play clothes. And I most heartily require the said Sir Thomas to be friendly unto Fulk Gillom & William Shakeshafte now dwelling with me & either to take them unto his service or else to help them to some good master, as my trust is he will ...

Four of the legatees, including Shakeshafte, were awarded £2 each; twenty-five of the thirty named legatees received less. This seems to show that he was especially valued and liked. The identification of 'all manner of play-clothes' suggests a wardrobe for theatricals. Alexander, having actors and musicians for his theatre, had musical instruments and stage clothes. The present Sir Bernard de Hoghton, Baronet, says that his father Sir Cuthbert de Hoghton (Twelfth Baronet) had seen them at Rufford Old Hall in the 1920s and 1930s. The Heskeths took them to Easton Neston, their home in Northamptonshire when Rufford was given to the National Trust; since then, they have disappeared.

Thomas's and Alexander's half-brother, mentioned in the above will, was also called Thomas, a son of his father's marriage to Alice Morley. He was murdered in a serious affray at Lea in 1589, which led Queen Elizabeth to ask Lord Derby to hold a 'special hearing', where the murderer saved his life by giving his Walton estates to the Hoghtons by way of forfeit.

As Honigmann asserts, 'it is highly unlikely that such a family would employ, at a time so dangerous for recusants, a servant who was not a practising Catholic.' (p. 9) Frank Singleton, in his guidebook to Hoghton Tower, writes:

In those days when the Jesuits travelled in secret from house to house, or hid in priest-holes behind the wainscot, Blessed Edmund Campion came, preached, and deposited his secret papers in the house for safe-keeping.

Alexander, when he dictated his will to his lawyer, knew that the Heskeths kept players, and that they would take and appreciate the instruments and play-clothes as additions to their own in the event that Thomas did not want them. This in practice is what appears to have happened.

What happened to Fulke Gyllom? According to Honigmann, he 'surfaces ten years later as a witness for Sir Thomas Hesketh's son Robert, and appears to have become attached to the Heskeths, together with Alexander's musical instruments' (p. 21). The Gylloms were Chester theatre people and were related to the Hathaways of Warwickshire.

What happened to 'William Shakeshafte'? He does not surface. Honigmann writes: 'in the hundreds of Hoghton and Hesketh documents I have examined, from the 1560s to the 1620s, I have come across no other trace of a 'servant' called William Shakeshafte.'

A plausible explanation is as follows: Alexander was not well; his mind was not what it was. He had a huge amount of detail concerning his family, his assets, his servants, retainers, and so on, that he had to deal with, and he put in this 'tontine' arrangement where cash asset is passed down the line as each legatee dies, so he had to name each one. He dictates his will and he gets some details wrong, understandably. When he comes to mention his servant William Shakespeare to his lawyer's scribe, he says 'Shakeshafte', in error, because this was a name he was familiar with. There were, and are, very many Shakeshaftes living in the north-west of England. There is a Shakeshafte Road in nearby Blackburn. The name 'Shakespeare' was probably unknown to him because it was not present in his community; it was not a common Lancashire name; it would be very rare here. It is a common and well-known name in Warwickshire, over a hundred miles from Lancashire and the Ribble, where dozens of families carried it then, and hundreds now. Undeniably, there is a close similarity between 'Shakespeare' and 'Shakeshafte'. A spear can be named as a shaft. The 'William' is common to both; the 'Shake' is common to both. That puts two-thirds of each name in the same form. The two names are significantly similar. Given all the other circumstances mentioned, especially the Cottom connection, the association of Shakespeare with 'Shakeshafte' is reasonable.

The prominent Catholic espouser Edmund Campion, before he was put to death at the end of 1581, spent time during the spring of the year in the household of Hoghton of Hoghton Tower. It is possible that the young William had met him.

If we accept the hypothesis, what happened then? Honigmann tells us that the unusual name of 'Fulk Gyllom' appears twice—in 1591 and 1608—in the Hesketh archives. So he moved on to work for the wealthy Heskeths. 'Shakeshafte' had lost his employer so he had to move on; possibly accompanying his friend Fulk.

What happened to the musical instruments? Sir Bernard has explained that they went on to Easton Neston with the Heskeths. Alan Keen had written in *The Annotator* (1954):

> Shortly after I reached this stage in my quest, Lord Hesketh found in his home, Easton Neston, some old musical instruments which were among household effects moved some years previously from Rufford. These may well be some of those catalogued in an inventory, now in the County records at Preston, of the goods of 'Robert Hesketh late of Rufforth' at 16 November 1620. The list of instruments includes 'vyolls, vyolentes, virginalls, sagbutts, howboies and cornets, cithron, flute and taber pypes'. An assortment that would have well suited a small stage orchestra. (p. 46)

Honigmann believes it possible that many of these instruments were sold off as 'junk' by the Hesketh family in the 1950s and 1960s.

Alan Keen says that he was told of 'the oral tradition that William Shakespeare had been at the Hall [Rufford] as a young man.' These oral traditions are sometimes true.

Rufford, the then seat of the Heskeths, is only twelve miles or so down the spine of Lancashire from Hoghton Tower and Lea Hall (which are about 9 miles apart). If a traveller crossed the Ribble by boat from Lea, the journey was quicker than by road through Preston.

A link between Shakespeare and Rufford was discovered by Alan Ken and Leslie Hotson. In 1599, Shakespeare and four colleagues acquired a half share in London's Globe Theatre. One of the two wealthy merchants who guided the arrangements was Thomas Savage. He was a native of Rufford and was related to the Heskeths of Rufford through marriage. The implication is that Shakespeare was at Rufford under the Heskeths and that Savage was an acquaintance. Stephen Greenblatt puts the status of these families in perspective:

> Will's life, if he actually sojourned in the north, would have been a peculiar compound of theatricality and danger. On the one hand, a life of open, exuberant display, where for the first time Will's talents—his personal charm, his musical skills, his power of improvisation, his capacity to play a role, and perhaps even his gifts as a writer—were blossoming in performances beyond the orbit of his family and friends. His performances would not have been exactly public, but neither were they simply private after-dinner entertainments. The Heskeths were immensely wealthy, while the Hoghtons and, still more, the Stanleys were feudal magnates. They were representatives of a world of riches, power and culture that had not yet been completely assimilated into a centralizing, hierarchical scheme of the Tudor monarchy, just as they had not yet been assimilated into the state religion.

Will in the World, p. 105

Sir Thomas Hesketh of Rufford was put under arrest in 1581 for his Catholic sympathies, and apparently again in 1584. If William Shakespeare was part of the household, as scribe, teacher, singing-master, and player-apprentice, he is likely to have stayed only a short time. As his theatrical interests and ambitions were rising, it may well be that he took advantage of the closeness between the Heskeths and Henry, the Fourth Earl of Derby, and joined the latter's retinue as a scribe, teacher and new player. He could have been noticed by Henry and his son and asked to join the Lathom enterprise, who were on the look-out for new players (and they got a writer as well).

In his will, Alexander Hoghton had asked Sir Thomas 'to be friendly' to Shakeshafte and, if necessary, to help him 'to come good master'. Honigmann writes:

> The obvious patron for Shakeshafte, in Sir Thomas's eyes, would be the Earl of Derby or Lord Strange, whose professional players were not home-based but toured the land ... there are good reasons for believing that William Shakespeare served in the 1580s as a retainer of Lord Strange ... Sir Thomas Hesketh could have recommended his talented player to Lord Strange in 1582.

4

Marriage, Children, and Early Writings

The first fact of our survey of the first third of Shakespeare's life was his birth. Fact two is his marriage. On 27 November 1582, a marriage licence was issued to Shakespeare and 'Annam Whateley de Temple Grafton'. Some writers have made much of what was almost certainly a scribal error in penning the bride's name, for she was undoubtedly Hathaway. Shakespeare's 'Sonnet 145' ('Those lips that Love's own hand did make') proves this, with puns on that name.

The whole poem is clearly an allusion to his relationship with Anne. Even though this is not a poem of high art—it has a flat rhythm, staccato diction, short lines, and a plodding pun on 'Hathaway'—it is significant simply because it is here. In its inclusion late in the series of 154 sonnets, the author appears not to want to complete his spiritual, ethical, and aesthetical biography without some token of appreciation of his early life with Anne.

Sams identifies poems Nos twelve, seventeen, and eighteen from the assorted collection *The Passionate Pilgrim* as from this period, involving a lovelorn shepherd in seventeen and a shepherd again in twelve ('Crabbed age and youth cannot live together'). Sams writes:

> No. 18 shares the iambic quadrimeter of Sonnet 145: 'when as thine eye hath chose the dame/ And stalled the deer that thou shouldst strike.' which reads like another Hathaway poem from the same period of deer-killing and courtship; indeed the two procedures are punningly equated by the dual idea of deer and dear, as also in 'dear deer' (*1 Henry VI*, IV.ii.54)

A woman whose maiden name was Hathaway was Shakespeare's bride of November 1582. William was eighteen years old.

Their daughter Susanna was christened at Holy Trinity Church Stratford on 26 May 1583; the inscription reads, 'Susanna, daughter to William Shakespeare'. When we take nine months backwards, we arrive at the month of August 1582, when Susanna was most likely conceived—William Shakespeare was courting Anne Hathaway at Stratford at this point in time. When they married, she was four months pregnant.

If the Lancashire Theory is correct as it has been presented here, given that he was at Lea during August 1581 when Alexander Hoghton dictated his will, his death following shortly, that chronology sees him leaving during September–December 1581, joining the Heskeths at Rufford, and getting to Stratford on or before August 1582. Such a procedure does not give him much time for courting Anne of Stratford.

This may add something to our understanding of what really went on. The thought is that if William had been in Stratford through the years say 1578 to 1582, between his fourteenth and eighteenth years, would a mature woman such as Anne Hathaway (some eight years his senior) be a likely match for him, or him for her? Would it not be more likely that over a year or two, he would have courted a girl of about his own age? Given the possibility that through most of the period 1579–82, William was in Lancashire (being a 'schoolmaster in the country' among other occupations), would not a brief relationship between a keen-to-marry Anne and the Stratford-visiting eighteen-year-old William seem more likely to fit the circumstances?

William and his new bride, the story goes, move in to live with his parents in their Henley Street home. Throughout 1583, John Shakespeare was absent from all fourteen recorded council meetings. His financial troubles and loss of local prestige continue.

On 2 February 1585, the twins, 'Hamnet and Judeth sonne and daughter to William Shakspere' are christened. They were named after Hamnet and Judith Sadler, residents of Stratford. Hamnet Sadler was one of the witnesses to Shakespeare's will of 1616.

Again, if we go nine months backwards, we arrive at a possible conception time in May 1584. So, we have the conception of Susanna in August 1582 and the conception of Hamlet and Judith in May 1584: there is a span of twenty-one months between these two—why so long?

It is likely that the new Mr and Mrs Shakespeare were financially embarrassed, especially given John Shakespeare's continuing difficulties, and that William badly needed an income, not only for himself, his wife, and their three children, but also for the rest of the household, his parents, and their children. It is very possible that at this fraught time, before and after the birth of twins, William was working for Henry, the Fourth Earl of Derby, at Lathom and Knowsley, Lancashire, helping with theatricals and teaching the children of his retainers, including the eldest daughter of his son Ferdinando, Lord Strange, Anne (b. 1580), who in 1585 was five years old.

Such a move to a very wealthy household where a regular income was guaranteed would be made possible by William's sympathy towards Catholicism; his pleasant, pliant, demeanour; his ability as a scribe (he could teach handwriting); his knowledge of the classics, including Latin; and his budding ability as an actor with a strong interest in theatricals. He could be very useful at the household of Earl Henry, the second richest person in England.

The period from February 1585 to February or March 1592 is the most problematical for the Shakespearean biographer or commentator. No information directly relating to his life and work is available. What we do know is that the financial fortunes of John and Mary Shakespare have not improved. On 19 January 1586, a writ was issued against John Shakespeare, but he had no goods on which distraint could be made. On 6 September 1586, he lost his position of alderman: 'At this Hall William Smythe and Richard Cowrte are chosen to be aldermen in the places of John Wheeler and John Shaxspere'; 'Mr. Shaxpere dothe not come to the halles when they be warned, nor hathe not done of long tyme'.

During September 1587, John and Mary Shakespeare offered to transfer the property Asbies (which had previously been mortgaged) to John Lambert for another twenty pounds: part of the deposition reads, 'Johannes Shackespere *et* Maria *uxor eius, simul cum* Willielmo Shackespere *filio suo*', proving that their talented son William was helping his parents with their financial and legal problems. Early in 1589, a bill of complaint was heard at Westminster against John Lambert on behalf of John and Mary Shakespeare and their son William. They alleged that in September 1587, they had been promised twenty pounds by John Lambert; he denied it. The suit for restoring the property was unsuccessful. These problems do not tell us where the son was or his precise role, but they do indicate the financial pressures his parents were subject to, their involvement with litigation and the supporting role played in these legal-financial affairs by their eldest son. A key element is the son's skill at handwriting and drafting.

In 1985, Eric Sams (with a doctorate from Cambridge and a career at the highest level of the British Civil Service) caused consternation among the vested interests of Shakespearean academics by publishing *Shakespeare's Edmund Ironside: The Lost Play*. His findings are still generally not accepted. His thesis was that this was a play entirely written by Shakespeare and that it was composed very early in his career. He writes the following in his introduction:

> This will surely be in some sense a rare book. It is an avowedly polemical and anything but diplomatic edition of the anonymous Tudor manuscript play *Edmund Ironside* which now stands fifth in the British Library collection Egerton 1994. I aim to show that *Ironside*, as I shall call it, is an early work by William Shakespeare, first written and acted *c.* 1588 ...

Sams asserted that the play preceded those more mature and more skilled plays included in the First Folio; he quoted with approval the words of John Wilder that Shakespeare 'did not simply burst into life as a fully-fledged dramatist.'

From the manuscript of the play *Edmund Ironside* (5th in the British Library Egerton 1994 collection). Eric Sams believed this was one of Shakespeare's first plays and that the handwriting could be his.

The handwritten manuscript of *Ironside* is the only manuscript extant carrying a play ascribed (albeit controversially) to Shakespeare. If the handwriting on it is Shakespeare's (holograph) then this is one of the most valuable manuscripts in the world. All the source manuscripts of First Folio plays have been lost. Elizabethans thought that handwritten manuscripts were of no value if the text had appeared in print, and they were re-used in cookery or as wrapping.

From a history plays perspective, note that Edmund Ironside (*c.* 981–1016) was King of the English (1016). He succeeded his father Ethelred the Unready. He fought the Danes under King Cnut.

In 1996, Eric Sams published Shakespeare's *Edward III: An Early Play Restored to the Canon* (Yale University Press). He writes in the introduction, 'At least one professional (Honigmann, 1982. 1985) has cogently contended that Shakespeare wrote his first plays before the accepted date of *c.* 1590, his twenty-sixth year.'

From our purpose, we note that the first scene involves the Earl of Derby, who is on stage but has nothing to say. In scene one, Prince Edward says, 'I hold thy message but as scurrilous/and him that sent thee like a lazy drone/crept up by stealth unto the eagle's nest'. This allusion can be seen as influenced by the Stanley family, whose Lathom HQ was referred to as 'the Eagle's Nest' on account of the family's emblem, an eagle's claw. Another eagle allusion appears in Act III, scene 1: 'puffed with rage/no otherwise than were their sails with wind/made forth as when the empty eagle flies/to satisfy his hungry, griping maw.'

Historically, Edward III (1312–77) was proclaimed King in 1327; he precipitated the Hundred Years War, claiming France as his. His achievements—military triumphs and domestic peace—were well regarded. In genealogy, he was the founder of the House of Lancaster. John of Gaunt (1340–99) was one of his sons. Henry IV (Bolingbroke) was son of John of Gaunt, and therefrom, Henry V (1387–1422) and Henry VI (1421–1471). Henry VII (Henry Tudor) (1457–1509) was descended from John of Gaunt's liaison with Catherine Swynford, so his claim to the throne of England was disputed. The Stanleys were blood-linked to this line of kings through Margaret Clifford, Henry the Fourth Earl's wife, being descended from Mary, Queen Dowager of France, who was Henry VII's eldest daughter. So, Ferdinando and William, sons of Earl Henry, could trace their ancestry back to John of Gaunt, not through the Bolingbroke line, but via the Earl of Somerset line, son of John of Gaunt and Catherine.

Shakespeare's (alleged) composition of the play *Edward III* can be seen as his first attempt to dramatise the Lancastrian line of kings, to be followed by *Henry VI* (parts one, two, and three) and the other five linked English history plays: these do not take in *King John* and *Henry VIII*. In this, he can be seen as creating oblique propaganda for the significant predecessors of the Tudor Queen Elizabeth (Henry VII's granddaughter), whom he wished to 'keep in with' and please, not least for the advancement of his theatrical career. His creation of his English History plays can be seen as designed to raise the profile of the Stanley family, whose Lancastrian cause they dramatise and whose Royal relatives they characterise.

5

Edmund Spenser:
Observer, Commentator, and
Rival Poet?

On Saturday, 13 January 1599. church bells tolled in Westminster. The news was shocking and depressing: Edmund Spenser was dead at the age of forty-six. Three days later Spenser was interred near Chaucer in the south transept of Westminster Abbey, in what would come to be known as 'Poets' Corner' … Spenser's hearse was 'attended by poets, and mournful elegies and poems, with the pens that wrote them, thrown into the tomb'. Camden added later that poets even carried Spenser's hearse … The verses, which the poets had but three days to compose, would have first been read aloud before being ceremoniously tossed into the grave. Not just a great poet was celebrated this day, but English poetry itself. It is unlikely that many of London's writers would have missed the occasion.

1599: A Year in the Life of William Shakespeare, James Shapiro, p. 80

Firstly, a few lines about the life and work of this famous poet, author of the long poem *The Faerie Queene,* one of the major poems of English Literature. He was born in or close to 1552, probably in East Smithfield, London, and was educated at Merchant Taylors' School and Pembroke Hall, Cambridge. In 1578, he obtained a position in the Earl of Leicester's household. In 1579, he started *The Faerie Queene* and published *The Shepherds Calendar*, his first important work, which was well received. He moved to Ireland in 1580 to take up an administrative appointment. He returned to London in 1589 with three books of *Faerie Queene*, which were prepared for the press, returning to Ireland in 1591; he penned his verse commentary 'Colin Clouts Come Home Again', printed in 1595. His poem 'The Tears of the Muses' was included in *Complaints, Containing sundry Small Poems of the World's Vanities,* published in 1591. In this, the poet deplores, through the mouth of several Muses, the decay of literature and learning and the lack of patronage. In 1596, further sections of *The Faerie Queen* were published when Spenser was in London. He returned to Ireland in 1597, where he was forced to flee for his life from his home with his wife and children. He died, in distress, in 1599, at a lodging in King Street, Westminster, London, and was buried in Westminster Abbey.

Edmund Spenser returned from Ireland at the instigation of Sir Walter Raleigh to present his first three books of *The Faerie Queen* to Queen Elizabeth. He 'remained in England for more than a year enjoying his fame, making friends with his brother poets, being entertained in country houses, and acknowledged by his kinswomen of Althorpe, Lady Carey, Lady Strange and Lady Monteagle' (Encyclopedia Britannica). These three cousins of Spenser were all relations of Ferdinando, Alice (Lady Strange) being his wife, the other two his sisters-in-law, one of whom, Anne, was married to another Stanley.

Eric Sams describes Spenser as 'a renowned and revered leading light on the London literary scene, and an outspoken public critic and indeed satirist of such circles' and says that he knew Shakespeare's work. Sams draws attention to an overlooked comment by Rowe: 'Men of the most delicate Knowledge and polite Learning [have admired Shakespeare] … amongst these was the incomparable Mr Edmund Spencer, who speaks of him in his "The Tears of the Muses", not only with the praises due to a good Poet, but even lamenting his absence with the tenderness of a Friend.' The lines Rowe had in mind are probably these:

> All these and all that els the Comick Stage
> With seasoned wit and goodly pleasance graced,
> By which mans life in his likest image
> Was limned forth, are wholly now defaced....
> And he, the man whom Nature selfe had made
> To mock her selfe and Truth to imitate,
> With kindly counter under mimick shade,
> Our pleasant Willy, ah! is dead of late;
> With whom all joy and jolly meriment
> Is also deaded and in dolour drent (11.199–210)

> … But that same gentle spirit, from whose pen
> Large streams of honnie and sweet nectar flowe,
> Scorning the boldness of such base-born men
> Which dare their follies forth so rashlie throwe,
> Doth rather choose to sit in idle cell
> Than so himselfe to mockerie to sell (11.217–22)

The early lines of the above passage are almost certainly a response to the death of the comedian Richard Tarleton in September 1588. However, the lines beginning 'And he ...' and the man behind lines 217–222 can with some confidence be identified as Shakespeare. The honey and nectar reference is a familiar one in descriptions of him and his work. The second theatrical person, after the death of Tarleton, is still with us, asserts Spenser, but is in retreat; he is presented as a well-known writer, not an actor. The phrase 'idle cell' suggests a room in a quiet, relaxed, place. These lines were written in 1590 or shortly before. They tell us how Spenser saw things; they do not tell us what Shakespeare really was doing. It is very likely that he was far from idle; that he was working on his writing; sitting in a 'cell', writing, possibly in Latham. They are consistent with the view that in the period 1587–91, Shakespeare was not living in London but was away 'in the country' working on his first plays and contributing to the fortunes of the Derby dynasty.

Shakespeare reappears in Spenser's 'Colin Clouts Come Home Again':

> *There also is (ah no, he is not now!)*
> *But since I said he is, he quite is gone'*
> *Amyntas quite is gone, and lies full low,*
> *Having his Amaryllis left to moan.*
> *Help, O ye shepherds, help ye all in this,*
> *Help Amaryllis this her loss to mourn:*
> *Her loss is yours, your loss Amyntas is,*
> *Amyntas, flower of shepherds' pride forlorn.*
> *He whilst he lived was the noblest swain,*
> *That ever piped piped in an oaten quill:*
> *Both did he other, which could pipe, maintain,*
> *And eke could pipe himself with passing skill.*
> *And there, though last not least, is Aetion,*
> *A gentler shepherd may nowhere be found:*
> *Whose Muse, full of high thought's invention,*
> *Doth like himself heroically sound.*

It is generally agreed by commentators that Amyntas is Ferdinando Stanley, who became the Fifth Earl of Derby in 1593 and who died in 1594. Amaryllis is his widow, Alice, to whom 'The Tears of the Muses' was dedicated. These lines are, of course, penned in the flattering language of patronage. The last four lines are almost undeniably an allusion to Shakespeare: his name has a heroic sound (shaking a spear heroically, say, in battle). Oddly, Honigmann seems to have missed the significance of the important word 'Aetion'. This derives from the Greek word for eagle. Here, the reference is to 'man of the eagle' or eaglet. The *Shorter Oxford English Dictionary* (Third Edition, 1959, p. 30) defines the derivative Aetites as 'the eagle-stone; a hollow nodule of argillaceous oxide of iron, having a loose nucleus, fabled to be found in the eagle's nest.' As the eagle was the emblem of the Stanleys, this allusion makes it plain that Spenser is asserting that Shakespeare was 'of' the Stanleys, that he was attached to them, part of their household and enterprise.

The eagle appears on the Stanley crest: designated 'eagle and child'; the motto is '*sans changer*'. Interestingly, when Shakespeare resumed his father's application for a Grant of Arms from the College of Heralds, the crest is: falcon and spear; the motto is '*non sans droit*'. In appearance, the designs are similar, with an eagle on one and a falcon on the other, and on each a coloured band from top left to bottom right, the one enclosing three stags' heads, the other enclosing a spear.

Another reference in the same poem, also missed by many commentators, lies in the line 'Both did he other, which could pipe, maintain'. This means that Ferdinando was a poet himself and he supported poets. The critical word here is 'maintain'. The *Oxford Dictionary*, p. 1,190, says: 'Maintain ... 6. To support (one's state in life) by expenditure, etc; to sustain life by nourishment. ME. 7 To provide with means of subsistence or necessaries of life. ME.' This 'support' meaning of 'maintain' was of course extant at the time of Spenser's writing. As this 'maintain' comes in a section devoted to Ferdinando and immediately before a reference to Shakespeare, it is clear that Spenser is telling us that Shakespeare was part of the Stanley entourage, that he was supported by them, and most likely 'employed' (in the modern sense, paid) by them.

Honigmann writes:

> Anyone who believes, as I do, that Shakespeare had written five history plays before the end of 1591 (the three parts of *Henry VI, Richard III* and *King John*) will conclude that Spenser referred to this astonishing achievement when he applauded a gentle shepherd's heroic muse ... Spenser, a shrewd observer of the literary scene, was almost certainly the first poet to write appreciatively of his great contemporary in print. (p. 76)

If we now step back and ask ourselves where Shakespeare was, we cannot disassociate this question from the observation: what was he doing and who was he doing it for? The answer is implicit in Honigmann's masterly analysis of the background of the early play *Love's Labour's Lost* (pp. 67–9):

> [This play] may be seen as a bantering comedy written for Lord Strange's entertainment by a privileged 'servant' who had observed Ferdinando over a period of years, and who knew what he could get away with ... The name Ferdinand survives in stage directions and speech prefixes in the quarto (which is thought to have been printed from Shakespeare's handwritten papers); the King of Navarre is never called Ferdinand in the dialogue ...

There is an argument for believing that Edmund Spenser is the 'rival poet' of Shakespeare's sonnets. The contentious beginning of Sonnet 86 has been much puzzled over: 'Was it the proud full sail of his great verse,/Bound for the prize of all too precious you'.

This seems to omit minor writers such as Barnabe Barnes and refer to one whom Shakespeare would regard as a major writer: Marlowe and Spenser are clear candidates, especially if we identify the 'you' in the above as Ferdinando, Lord Strange, whom both courted as patrons. Spenser's *The Faerie Queene* (1590 for Books I, II, and III) may well be the 'great verse' alluded to. His sailing to and from Ireland may be the origin of the sea imagery.

Ferdinando could be the central male figure of sonnets 75–90. In Sonnet 76, we have: 'Why with the time do I not glance aside/To new-found methods, and to compounds strange?' This could refer to the 'School of Night', a group of nobles, including the Fourth and Fifth Earls of Derby and Sir Walter Raleigh, who were interested in the new sciences, including astrology/astronomy and alchemy (note the words 'methods' and 'compounds'). The phrase 'school of night' occurs in *Love's Labour's Lost*, Act 4, Scene III, l. 266.

The word 'strange' is an interesting one; it occurs again in Sonnet 89: 'I will acquaintance strangle and look strange,/Be absent from thy walks, and in my tongue/Thy sweet beloved name no more shall dwell.' This points to leaving the household and influence of Lord Strange and going to live elsewhere, possibly to London in 1592 when his first plays were performed there.

Sonnet 80 begins:

> *O how I faint when I of you do write,*
> *Knowing a better spirit doth use your name,*
> *And in the praise thereof spends all his might,*

Edmund Spenser was distantly related to Alice (Spencer), Ferdinando's wife, so in a sense Spenser 'doth use your name'; and Spenser did spend time with the Derbys (they had a house in London), referring to them in his verse and dedicating 'The Tears of the Muses' (1591) to Alice.

Shakespeare's Sonnet 87 includes the following:

> *Farewell, thou art too dear for my possessing, ...*
> *So thy great gift, upon misprision growing,*
> *Comes home again, on better judgement making.*

The 'farewell' comment is in a group of sonnets (75–93) addressed (I propose) to Ferdinando and Spenser. 'Thy great gift' is Spenser's. The 'misprision' is between Spenser and Ferdinando, who are having a falling out, and Spenser is losing Ferdinando as a patron. Spenser is identified by 'Comes home again', which echoes his poem 'Colin Clouts Come Home Again' (1591) and the unusual word 'misprision'.

The phrase 'upon misprision growing' is so odd that the word 'misprision' deserves close examination. We find it in the *Shorter Oxford English Dictionary* (Little, Onions; third edition, 1959) Volume 1, p. 1,261:

> Obsolete: Misprize 1485 1. To commit an offence. 2. To mistake, misunderstand -1567
>
> 2. Monsieur Gaspar ... misprise me not B. JONS.
>
> 3. Hence (obs) Misprize sb 2 mistake SPENSER

When we follow this word, we find that 'misprize(d)' is used six times in the *Faerie Queene*, twice in Book II and once each in Books III, IV, and V.

It is very likely that Shakespeare noticed this word in the first publication of *The Faerie Queene* of 1590. He used it in six plays subsequently, all from the 1590s.

James Shapiro (p. 80) draws attention to the difference between Shakespeare's *metier* and that of Spenser. 'Spenser, after all, had chosen paths Shakespeare had rejected. He had pursued his poetic fortune exclusively through aristocratic— even royal—patronage, and had done so in':

> *... descriptions of the fairest wights,*
> *And beauty making beautiful old rhyme*
> *In praise of ladies dead and lovely knights.*

> Sonnet 106, Shakespeare

Following the theme of 'the dramatist's company allegiance' Honigmann writes, 'Apart from these apparent allusions to Lord Strange and his family in *Richard III* and *Love's Labour's Lost*, there are others in *Henry VI*, Parts 2 and 3, and in *A Midsummer Night's Dream* that I think are intriguing ...' (p. 69)

Professor Honigmann summarises: 'Shakespeare, I repeat, seems to have served Lord Strange for eight or more years—the crucial years of his apprenticeship in the theatre.'

The years between 1582 and 1592 would be made up of two different time periods. Firstly, there were times when he worked for Lancashire Catholic families, notably the Stanleys: these were his 'business' periods, in Lancashire. Then, secondly, there are the domestic times—his 'family' periods—in Stratford, spent courting, marrying, fathering children, looking after the household in Henley Street, and helping his father with his financial problems.

6

'Matchless Navarre': Ferdinando, Heir to the Throne, Poisoned

Ferdinando, Lord Strange, eldest son of Henry, the Fourth Earl of Derby, was, as we have said, through his mother Margaret Clifford and his grandmother Eleanor Brandon, a great-great-grandson of Henry VII. Henry Tudor was the only son of Edmund Tudor, Earl of Richmond, and Margaret Beaufort, whom Thomas Stanley married shortly after the death of her second husband Henry Stafford.

> Lady Margaret Beaufort was descended from John of Gaunt, Duke of Lancaster by his relationship with Katherine Swynford whom he later married. The children of this relationship were legitimized by Henry 1V but he excluded a right to the throne. Henry Tudor had been brought up in the household of William Herbert, Earl of Pembroke ... and fled to France in July 1469 ...
>
> Jean M. Gidman, *Sir William Stanley of Holt*, p. 12

Ferdinando was a cousin of Queen Elizabeth, and, Ian Wilson says, 'with the failure of the male Tudor line, a more than possible candidate to succeed Elizabeth on the English throne.' (p. 107)

Ferdinando was summoned to Parliament as Lord Strange in January 1588–9, in the lifetime of his father, the Fourth Earl, and was (see *D. N. B.* vol. L1V.67) 'a patron and friend of many poets of the time and was himself a writer of verses and patron of the company of actors formerly under the patronage of the Earl of Leicester'.

Ian Wilson's Catholicism asserts itself:

> Of one thing there can be no doubt: for the sizeable number of English Catholics who had fled abroad to escape government persecution, not to mention any unspoken feelings of those back home, Ferdinando was a distinctly credible hope as Elizabeth's successor. Equally definite is that

Ferdinando Stanley, 5th Earl of Derby (1559?–1594) (1594).

Elizabeth's first minister Lord Burghley and his cohort of spies and secret agents held Ferdinando in the deepest distrust.

In 1586, the Babington Plot was uncovered. One of the conspirators (who was hanged, drawn, and quartered at Tyburn Hill, London) was Thomas, elder brother of John Salusbury of Denbigh and heir to his mother Catrin of Berain's Tudor inheritance. Berain was, and is, a house and land some 3 miles west of St Asaph, Denbighshire. Three months later, John married Ursula, Ferdinando's half-sister. She moved from Hawarden Castle, her father's occasional residence on the Wales–England border to the west of Chester, to live in the Salusbury mansion, Lleweni, near Denbigh, some 20 miles distant.

Ferdinando, given the equivocation of his father Henry towards anti-Catholicism, badly needed to assert and display his loyalty to Protestantism and the Queen.

As Wilson points out, Ferdinando was an enthusiastic horse-and-tilt-man; he rode for Her Majesty at the Whitehall Tilts 1589–92. George Peele describes him:

> *The Earl of Derby's valiant son and heir,*
> *Brave Ferdinand Lord Strange, strangely embarked*
> *Under Jove's kingly bird, the golden Eagle,*
> *Stanley's old crest and honourable badge ...*

Wilson continues:

> But could yet another way of Ferdinando's showing his loyalty to Elizabeth—whatever its sincerity—have been by commissioning from Shakespeare and his crew the spectacle of *Henry VI/Richard III*? By presenting in dramatised form the events of the Wars of the Roses, with all its horrors of great lords struggling over royal succession, could Ferdinand have been demonstrating his distaste for such *lese-majeste*? By reviving Richard III and his murder of the princes, could Ferdinand have been presenting a subtle warning to Elizabeth of the fate of tyrants who shed the blood royal? By re-enacting that moment of all moments, when none other than Ferdinando's own great-great-great-grandfather had set the crown of England upon the head of Henry Tudor, might Ferdinando not have wanted to remind Elizabeth that it was to a loyal Stanley that she owed her crown?

Shakespeare: The Evidence, p. 110

This is very well put. Ferdinando possessed the resources: 'an acting company with its own promising new dramatist.' Wilson points out that during the winter of 1591–1592, the court accounts record Lord Strange's Men performing for the Queen six productions at Whitehall between 27 December and 8 February; unfortunately, the titles of the plays are not recorded.

Shakespeare needed source books for his history plays. Where did he get them from? He was financially poor before 1595. The books were expensive and only the well-off could afford them. His will of 1616 said nothing about owning books. Where might the volumes be available to him so that he could gut their contents for his play material? One answer is in the libraries of the grand houses. The Stanley family owned four houses, one in London. In one or two of these, there would be a fine library, the volumes bound in leather in the livery of choice. These were, most likely, at Lathom, Lancashire, and in Derby House in Cannon Row, London (the city where printing and publishing took place and where new books were bought). We have already touched on the extraordinary story of Alan Keen, antiquarian bookseller of London, finding an old copy of Halle's *Chronicle* (a key text for these history plays), which was heavily annotated. In the next chapter, we shall evoke this in detail. Another of his sourcebooks, North's translation of Plutarch was once owned by the Stanleys (see Chapter 14).

However strong his connections, Ferdinando never came to the throne of England. Elizabeth, surrounded by devoted and ruthless courtiers, survived as sovereign into old age, and when she died, the Tudor line expired.

In 1593, on 25 September, Henry, the Fourth Earl of Derby, died at Lathom, Lancashire, the ancestral home. It is reported that on the same day, one of the nobility of Lancashire arrived at Lathom Richard Hesketh from London. He carried a letter inviting Ferdinando to be a figurehead in a Catholic plot to overthrow the Queen. It was explosive stuff. Ferdinando took Hesketh and the letter straight to the Queen in London. He could not be sure that it was not a plot by her advisors to test his loyalties. The Queen took swift measures and the unfortunate Hesketh was executed at St Albans on 29 November.

Dover Wilson is convinced that *Love's Labour's Lost* was written to be performed for private performance at Christmas 1593:

> It is my belief that in Ferdinand, King of Navare, Berowne … , the spectators were intended to see stage-reflections—not, of course, portraits—of Ferdinando Stanley, who had become Earl of Derby and King of Man in September 1593, [and] the Earl of Essex who had been fighting side by side with Biron, or as the English called him, Berowne, on French soil in 1591 [and] Southampton himself.

> *The Essential Shakespeare*, p. 66

On 4 April 1594, at Knowsley, Ferdinando fell ill. He was vomiting, although well enough to ride to Lathom the next day. He had blood in his vomit and in his urine; he developed jaundice and his kidneys failed. By 11 April, he realised he was dying, and he made his will. He kept his brother William out of it. He left his entire estate to his wife, Countess Alice, and after her death, to his eldest daughter Anne. On 16 April 1594, Ferdinando died. The cause of death, according to Ian Wilson, was almost certainly arsenic poisoning, 'administered in a single, highly lethal dose'. He was buried at Ormskirk. *Burke's Peerage* remarks that Ferdinando 'is supposed to have been poisoned in consequence by the conspirators'.

Elizabeth, it is reported, grieved, saying that 'he was the most honourable, worthiest and absolutely honest man that she had in her life ever known'. Whether this is to be believed is anybody's guess. Who administered the poison and why? Was it somebody set on avenging the Hesketh death? Or does suspicion fall on the other side, the anti-Catholics in the Court of Elizabeth, who perhaps believed that Ferdinando's apparent anti-Catholicism was only a cover? However, a Protestant succession was assured.

At the time of Earl Ferdinando's death, he had three daughters but no son: his brother William was therefore heir presumptive in the succession. However, Ferdinando's widow (Dowager Countess Alice, who later married Lord Ellesmere) was then—allegedly—pregnant and it would not be known for some time whether a posthumous son might be born. Yet no fourth child was born (a stillbirth is a possibility) and William's presumptive title accrued. He succeeded to the earldom and became involved in lengthy litigation regarding his acquisitions, instigated by Alice.

Edmund Spenser grieved over the death of the Fifth Earl, Ferdinando; he had lost a patron. He revised the manuscript of 'Colin Clout', inserting the sad epitaph to 'Amyntas'.

Shakespeare was in serious trouble. He had lost his theatricals patron. Yet his 'poetry patron' was intact, the young, wealthy Earl of Southampton. He had already written his long narrative poem *Venus and Adonis* and dedicated it to the Earl. Now somewhat desperate to secure and keep this patronage, he finished another long poem, *The Rape of Lucrece*, dedicating it to the Earl with an even more colourful preamble: 'The love I dedicate to your Lordship is without end … what I have done is yours, what I have to do is yours'. This was entered at Stationers' Register, London (a device for securing copyright) on 9 May 1594.

However, Shakespeare's luck was turning. After a short period under dowager Alice, his theatrical troupe found a new patron, the elderly Henry Carey, Lord Hunsdon. He became Lord Chamberlain and from June 1594, Alice's short-lived acting troupe was re-named 'The Lord Chamberlain's Men' with William Shakespeare as their chief playwright and part-owner ('sharer'). They were later to become 'The King's Men'. The Public Record Office, London, have a record of a payment made in March 1595 'To William Kemp, William Shakespeare and Richard Burbage servants to the Lord Chamberlain'. This is the first time Shakespeare's name is linked with any acting company. The fact that his name is alongside two known members of the old Lord Strange's or Earl of Derby's company is some indication of a putative link with that company.

7

Alan and Frances Keen:
Book Dealers and
Lancashire Investigators

The volume *The Annotator* (Putnam, 1954) is essential reading for anyone interested in the Lancashire Theory. It details not only the chance discovery of an important old book but continues the investigation well beyond the boundaries of the book and its annotations. It moves into Lancashire territory and has laid the groundwork for further research.

The story begins in wartime London, in June 1940. Alan Keen refers to the aircraft in the skies as he settles down in his office to look at an old book, which has just been lifted out of a 'shabby portfolio'. It was Edward Halle's (1498–1547) *The Union of the Two Noble and Illustre Famelies of Lancastre and Yorke*, a history of the period 1399–1532. He says that the title page was missing but he gives the reader what it should have read; he characterises this page's text as 'the opening fanfare of the Tudor historian':

> The union of the two noble and illustrate famelies of Lancastre & Yorke, beyng long in continuall discension for the croune of this noble realme, with all the actes done in both the tymes of the Princes, both of the one linage & of the other, beginnyng at the tyme of kyng Henry the fowerth, the first aucthor of this devision, and so successively proceading to ye reigne of the high and prudent Prince Kyng Henry the eyght, the indubitate flower and very heire of both the saied linages.

Who was Halle? He was, according to Halliday in his invaluable *A Shakespeare Companion* (Penguin Books, 1964), a member of a staunchly Protestant Shropshire family, educated at Eton and King's, read law at Grey's Inn, and entered Parliament.

> His *The Union* ... was written to glorify the Tudors and to show 'that as by discord great thynges decaie and fall to ruine, so the same by concord be revived and erected'. The second issue of 1548 contained the addition of

Richard Grafton, printer and chronicler, who himself added the history of
the years 1532–47. Halle, rather than Holinshed, was Shakespeare's main
source for his early histories, and he observed Halle's moral pattern of the
discord following the overthrow of the established order being resolved by its
restoration. (p. 203)

Keen saw that many of the early pages of his book had handwritten notes in the
margins. He took the book to the British Museum and had the ink subjected
to infrared and ultraviolet tests. They proved that the ink was 'of considerable
antiquity and were probably made all about the same time.' The book's original
owner was Rychard Newport; the year 1565 is handwritten next to initials of
his name.

A handwriting expert, examining the plentiful annotations, pointed out the
following to Keen:

It consists of exactly that mixture of Gothic and Roman forms, predominantly
Gothic, which was characteristic of the hand of Shakespeare and his
contemporaries. It is basically the provincial 'secretary cursive' hand used by
Shakespeare in his signatures, and by the scribe of the manuscript section of
'Sir Thomas More', said by some to be Shakespeare's.

Keen writes:

The annotator penned laborious notes running to three thousand six hundred
words, carefully extracting the pith and pattern of Halle's history, signposting
details for easy reference, and only very rarely expressing his own views ...
Our student seems to have been torn between sympathy with Halle's patriotic
enthusiasm and fury at his anti-Catholicism, but he did not let his personal
opinions intrude upon his thorough study: he made four hundred and six
marginal notes, as well as sundry crosses and underlinings, and only some
twenty-four of the notes can be considered in any way as comment. He never
cites another authority: as he shows himself to be studious, intelligent, and a
persistent annotator, one surmises that this was his first reading of the subject
... These notes appear to be the signposts left by a thoughtful and methodical
reader, who was planning to use a selection of the material for some purpose
of his own ... he was a patriot, and hated the French ... he had a strong
Roman Catholic, even clerical, bias. 'Allways lying,' he said of another tirade
of Halle's against 'proud priors'.
    ... An interesting point about these 'religious' comments is that most of
them have been either written over previous erasures (possibly still stronger
in tone) or half-heartedly obscured by A's own pen. Did he repent of them, or
was it simply natural caution in an age when recusants went to the stake?

PLATE II

appaired, foz he had onely two.ꝟ.hozſemen and.ruj.ꝟ. Archers, but men and of all ſoztes. The Engliſhemen were afflicted in this iourney with an hundred diſcoinodities, foz their bitaile was in maner al ſpent, and newe they could gette none, foz their enemies had deſtroyed all the cozne befoze their compny: Reſt they could take none, foz theyz enemies wer euer at hande, daily it reined and nightly it freſed, of fuell was ſkarcenes and of fluces was plenty, money they had ynough but comfozte ther had none. And yet in this greate neceſſitee the poze folkes wer not ſpoyled noz any thyng wythout paiment was of the extozted, noz great offence was doen except one, whiche was that a fooliſhe ſouldier ſtale a pice out of a chutche and vnreuerently did eate the holy hoſtes with in theſame conteigned. Foz whiche cauſe he was apprehended, and the kyng would not once remoue till the veſſel was reſtozed ⁊ the offender ſtrangled. The people of the countrees there aboute hearyng of hys ſtraight iuſtice ⁊ godly mynd, miniſtered to hym bothe bitailes ⁊ other neceſſaries, although by open pzoclamaciō they wer therof pzohibited.

1. *A section of H.v. f.xva. The note, 'A cryme committyd and if this boke had had one author it wold not have bene noted/nam oportet mendacem esse memorem', is referred to in Ch. II. The 'doodle' in the opposite margin, possibly referring to the 'foolishe souldier', is referred to in Appendix X.*

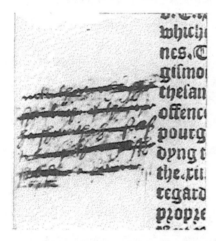

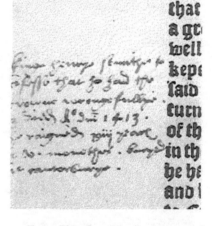

2. *One of the overscored notes referred to in Ch. II. From H.v. f.iiia, 'note that when he speakethe of the pope he shewithe himself to be of the englisshe schisme a favorer.'*

3. *From H.iv. f.xxxiii, shewing use of roman and arabic numerals. 'Kinge henrye semithe to confesse that he had the crowne wrongefullye and died Ao dni 1413. he raigned xiii yeares and v monethes. buryed at canterburye.'*

SOME ANNOTATIONS

A page from *The Annotator* by Keen and Lubbock showing Roman and Arabic numerals. The handwriting is secretary-style: small, clear, and strongly inked.

PLATE VII

1. *A signature of William Shakespeare, 1613. Note abrupt termination of the long 's'.*

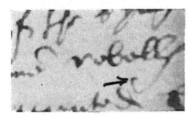   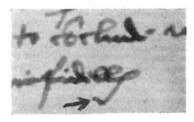

2. *'Rebells' from H.v.f.xii.*   3. *'Infidells' from H.iv.f.xxxii.*

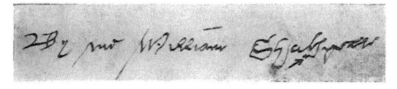

4. *Signature on p. 3 of 1616 will. Again note the jerky tail of the long 's'.*

5. *Signature on p. 2 of 1616 will. Note overlapping of 'll'.*

COMPARISON OF HANDWRITING
(*See Appendix iii*)

A page from *The Annotator* showing a comparison of the marginalia with William Shakespeare's signature on his will.

The annotator jots down a jingle 'he that wille scotland wynne let him with france first begynne'. This appears in Shakespeare's *Henry V* (Act I, scene 2, line 167), as 'If that you will France win/Then with Scotland first begin.'

Halle describes how before Agincourt the King had sharp-ended stakes driven into the ground so that they would catch attacking horses. Against this passage, the annotator had written, 'The inventyng of stakes which now I think be morres pykes'. Keen points out that Morris or Moorish pikes were sixteenth-century weapons of the type Halle describes but Halle does not use this name. The annotator uses the name. The name appears in a play by Shakespeare, in *A Comedy of Errors* (Act IV, scene 3, line 25), making Dromio of Syracuse speak of one who 'sets up his rest to do more exploits with his mace than a morris-pike'.

In the early play of Shakespeare's *Love's Labour's Lost*, Boyet (4.1) reads out to the Princess a letter from the fantastic Armado: 'The magnanimous and most illustrate King Cophetua set eye upon the pernicious and indubitate beggar Zenelophon' ... 'I am much deceived but remember this style', remarks Boyet. The style is very much that of Halle, whose opening words were, 'The Union of the two noble and illustr(at)e famelies of Lancastre and Yorke ... proceading to the reigne of the High and prudent Prince King Henry the Eighth, the indubitate and very heire of the said linages'.

Here is another extraordinary parallel. Biondello, in Shakespeare's *The Taming of the Shrew*, says 'Take you assurance of her "*cum privilegio ad imprimendum solum*" to the church; take the priest, clerk, and some sufficient honest witnesses.' This Latin expression appears under the imprint line in a book of 1550 printed by Richard Graften, the Halle printer.

Keen goes on:

> Another minute but telling supporter of the theory that Shakespeare was sometimes writing with Halle open beside him comes from the misprint where Halle has '..betwene the riuers of Elue and Sala', Holinshed gets the river right, Elbe; but Shakespeare apparently follows Halle in his error, and the First Folio text (the true text for *Henry V*) has 'Betweene the Flouds of sala and of Elue'. Professor Dover Wilson, in his preface to the play, concedes this as a pointer to the direct use of Halle.

After a number of other parallelisms, Keen believes that the annotator could have been Shakespeare. He asks the pertinent questions, 'But how could this copy of the "Chronicle" have come into Shakespeare's hands? Where was the book when A.[his shorthand for the annotator] made his notes? Or where was Shakespeare, if and when he made them?'

Keen says that the original owner of the volume, Richard Newport, was Sir Richard Newport, Lord Ercall and Sheriff of Shropshire, who died in 1570. He had written his name twice in the blank margins; on another leaf, he had put his initials with the date, '6 Apll. Ao 1565'. Keen writes:

> He had married Margaret, daughter and sole heir of Sir Thomas Bromley, Lord Chief Justice of England, and thus became owner of the great house at Eyton-on-Severn. Magdalen his daughter married Richard Herbert of Montgomery. She became a patroness of literature and a friend of John Donne … the families of Corbet, Newport, Bromley, Leveson, Vernon, Fitton, Arden, Holcroft and Hesketh were interrelated in a pattern which spread out from Shropshire to Lancashire … Richard Newport's possessions might have found their way into the homes of any of the families in this clan.

Keen, however, asserts later (on page 93) that the name Worsley inscribed in the volume has importance, and that the volume may have belonged to this family. He found a connection with the Newport family through two marriages. Robert Worsley married Elizabeth, second daughter of Sir Thomas Gerard of Bryn. Her sister was married to Thomas Hoghton, the elder brother of Alexander Hoghton of Lea. Keen speculates that the volume could have been at Lea or Hoghton Tower in 1579–1581, when the Lancashire Theory places the young Shakespeare, as 'Shakeshafte', there.

We do not know where this volume is now as it has disappeared. Mrs Marian J. Pringle, erstwhile special collections librarian of the Shakespeare Birthplace Trust, said: 'Everybody's looking for it. It's probably in the library of some private collector and he's keeping quiet about it.'

8

The First History Plays of Shakespeare, Staged in London in 1592

Shakespeare had determined to write a historical epic, like Marlowe's, but to make it an English epic, an account of the bloody time of troubles that preceded the order brought by the Tudors. He wanted to resurrect a whole world, as Marlowe had done, bringing forth astonishing larger-than-life figures engaged in struggles to the death, but it was now not the exotic realms of the East that would be brought to the stage but England's own past. The great idea of the history play—taking the audience back into a time that had dropped away from living memory but that was still eerily familiar and crucially important—was not absolutely new, but Shakespeare gave it an energy, power and conviction that it had never before possessed. The Henry VI plays are still crude, especially in comparison with Shakespeare's later triumphs in the same genre.

Stephen Greenblatt, *Will in the World*, p. 195

It seems from all the evidence that Shakespeare was not spending much time in, certainly not resident in, London before early 1592. If he had been there, his name would most likely have come up in sundry tax-collectors' lists, playing records, the Queen's court records, litigation accounts, church records, and suchlike, but it does not. Neither do we see that he was resident in Stratford. So, where was he? One thing we can be sure of: he was writing, as Edmund Spenser says. He was writing *Titus Andronicus* and he was certainly writing the 'minor tetralogy': the four English history plays, being the three parts of *Henry VI* and *Richard III*.

The earliest reliable reference we have to any play by Shakespeare staged in public is in the form of three allusions in 1592 to two of the three *Henry VI* plays staged in a London commercial public theatre. Firstly, on 3 March of that year, the theatrical entrepreneur Philip Henslowe recorded earnings of £3 16s 8d (a very good return) for a performance of 'harey the vi' by Lord Strange's

Men at the Rose Theatre. Secondly, Thomas Nashe's little book *Piers Penniless*, written August 1592 (see Sams, *The Real Shakespeare*, p. 73) argued that stage plays then were 'borrowed out of our English chronicles'; and he goes on, 'in the tragedian that represents [Talbot's] person, [they] image that they behold him fresh bleeding!' The only Talbot we know on the Elizabethan era stage is the one in Shakespeare's *1 Henry VI*. Nashe notes the popularity of *Henry VI*: 'ten thousand spectators at least, at several times' in the period March to May 1592.

The third contemporary reference to Shakespeare is a famous one by Robert Greene, playwright, written shortly before his death in September 1592. He sneeringly singles out an 'upstart crow' who 'beautified with our feathers, that with his "Tygers hart wrapt in a players hyde", supposes he is well able to bombast out blank verse as the best of you: and being an absolute *Johannes fac totum*, is in his own conceit the only Shake-scene in the country' (See Sams, *RS*, p. 217). This is clearly aimed at denigrating the new theatre man Shakespeare. The 'tygers hart ... players hyde' quip is an allusion to a remark in Shakespeare's *3 Henry VI*. Clearly annoyed and envious, ever since the mid-1580s, Greene had been seeking Stanley patronage. He had dedicated a play to Countess Margaret and another to Ferdinando.

So, before September 1592, it is probable that Shakespeare's *Henry VI*, Parts I and III, were staged in the commercial London theatre. It is also most likely that Part II was staged also, making the sequence. They attracted huge audiences. William Shakespeare, playwright, had—as they say—arrived.

In his book *The Earls of Derby 1485–1985*, J. J. Bagley writes:

> In these early historical plays it is noticeable how he emphasised the role played by the Stanley family. In *Henry VI, Part 2* Sir John Stanley is given the task of conveying the arrested Duchess of Gloucester to the Isle of Man; in 'Part 3', Edward IV gratuitously makes the point of promising a reward to Sir William Stanley; and in *Richard III* Thomas Stanley is the one who warns Hastings of the danger he is in, and is the chief instigator of the Richmond invasion. (p. 74)

Henry VI of England had a paternal great-grandfather in John of Gaunt (from Ghent, his birthplace), founder of the House of Lancaster and First Duke of Lancaster. Henry's paternal great-grandmother was John's wife, Blanche of Lancaster.

The 'major tetralogy', it is generally agreed, was written 1595–1599. These are: *Richard II*; *Henry IV Parts 1 and 2*; and *Henry V*.

The minor tetralogy (the three *Henry VI* plays and *Richard III*) deals with the English defeat by France in the last years of the Hundred Years War (enacted in *1 Henry VI*) followed by the disputes and battles of the English civil conflict, the Wars of the Roses. This tetralogy begins with the death of Henry V in 1422 and ends with the foundation of the Tudor Dynasty in 1485, at the Battle of Bosworth. The two tetralogies, generally, cover English history from 1398 to 1485.

In the cogent words of Boyce:

Shakespeare plunged into the disorder of the civil war in the first four plays and then, in the second, delved into the history that preceded this cataclysm, examining its causes and painting a portrait of the nation as it changed, traumatically, from medieval to modern. The central theme of these plays is political—they deal with the gain and loss of power—but Shakespeare transcended this subject. As he wrote his histories, the playwright increasingly pursued the definition of the perfect king. After presenting two distinctly bad rulers, the ineffectual Henry VI and the villainous Richard III, he turned to a consideration of kingly virtues ...

That secular accounts of the past, neither legendary nor religious, were presented on stage—and were highly popular—reflects the Elizabethan era's intense interest in history. In the late 16th century, when these plays were written, England was undergoing a great crisis. As a leading Protestant state, it found itself at odds with the great Catholic powers of Counter-Reformation Europe, including its traditional enemy, France, and a new foe, Spain. The latter, at the height of its power, was a very dangerous adversary, and England felt seriously imperilled until the defeat of the Spanish Armada in 1588. This situation sparked a tremendous patriotism among all classes of English society, and with that came an increasing interest in the nation's history, an interest that the theatre was of course delighted to serve ... the Wars of the Roses were the great crisis that had formed the nation, as Shakespeare and his contemporaries knew it. Its resolution at Bosworth Field lay in the relatively recent past. Thus Elizabethans were very much aware of the significance of the events depicted in these plays ... The English of the late 16th century felt a strong fear of civil war and anarchy; for both moral and practical reasons they valued an orderly society ruled by a strong monarch. The history plays addressed this attitude by presenting a lesson in the evils of national disunity ...

Encyclopedia of Shakespeare, pp. 294–295

In writing these history plays, Shakespeare had his finger on the pulse of the nation. He seldom wrote a play that did not in some way contain and reflect current concerns. Behind the history plays is the shadow of the personality and actions of the first Tudor king, Henry VII. The powerful dynamic contrast between kings Henry VI and Richard III, representing the perils of unstable medievalism contrasted with the brave and quietly efficient Henry VII, who laid down the groundwork of the modern British state, reverberates through the plays. The Battle of Bosworth, 1485, is the watershed—a turning-point in British history, when Henry Tudor (grandfather of Elizabeth I) came to power and brought stability, order and a sense of unified statehood: in Halle and Shakespeare's word, harmony. That, at least, is the propaganda.

In *3 King Henry VI*, there is a moment in Act 4, Scene 6, when the verse turns to such a note of conviction and beauty, that future resolution and peace under Henry VII seems secured.

> King Henry
>> My Lord of Somerset, what youth is that
>> Of whom you seem to have so tender care?
>
> Somerset
>> My liege, it is young Henry, Earl of Richmond.
>
> King Henry
>> Come hither, England's hope.
>> (Lays his hand on Richmond's head.)
>> If secret powers
>> Suggest but truth to my divining thoughts,
>> This pretty lad will prove our country's bliss.
>> His looks are full of peaceful majesty,
>> His head by nature framed to wear a crown,
>> His hand to wield a sceptre, and himself
>> Likely in time to bless a regal throne.
>> Make much of him, my lords, for this is he
>> Must help you more than you are hurt by me.

This beautiful passage describes the child Henry Tudor, only son of Margaret Beaufort, who married Thomas Stanley. Jean M. Gidman writes in her book *Sir William Stanley of Holt*:

> Her marriage to Thomas Stanley would appear to be a retrograde one in the sense that by it she became Lady Stanley as her husband was a Baron. She could have aspired to a nobler rank. The Stanleys, however, were a powerful family in the north-west of England, the two brothers [William and Thomas] holding estates in Lancashire and Cheshire as well as in North Wales. Perhaps it was this Welsh connection that gave her the incentive to marry into the family. With her son's own Welsh ancestry he could claim support from both North and South Wales. (p. 23)

Coleridge described *Richard II*, written as part of the second tetralogy, 1595–1596, as the most historical of Shakespeare's plays. Take two character sketches. First, consider that of the chief Lancastrian protagonist (Duke of Lancaster 1340–1399) at the opening page of the history series before the House of Lancaster succeeded to the throne. Old John of Gaunt, uncle to the King, says on his dying bed to the Duke of York:

Will the King come that I may breathe my last
In wholesome counsel to his unstaid youth?
[Gaunt then talks as in soliloquy]
Methinks I am a prophet new inspired
And thus expiring I do foretell of him.
His rash fierce blaze of riot cannot last,
Consuming means, son preys upon itself.
This royal throne of kings, this scept'red isle,
This earth of majesty, this seat of Mars,
This other Eden, demiparadise
This fortress built by Nature for herself
Against infection and the hand of war,
This happy breed of men, this little world,
This precious stone set in the silver sea
Which serves it in the office of a wall
Or as a moat defensive to a house
Against the envy of less happier lands;
This blessed plot, this earth, this realm, this England.

Was this famously partisanal passage written with a fortress-like house—a castle—in mind, with tall walls and a moat? Perhaps Lathom? Gaunt then goes on to say how the realm has been brought down from that ideal:

... This dear dear land,
Dear for her reputation through the world,
Is now leased out, (I die pronouncing it),
Like to a tenement or pelting farm,
... and bound in shame.
Ah! would the scandal vanish with my life
And happy then were my ensuing death.

Consider in contrast to that, the soliloquy of the later Duke of York who led the Yorkists to enthrone Edward IV in succession to the three Henrys—IV, V, and VI—which is in the opening scene of the second part of *Henry VI*:

Cold news for me; for I had hope of France
Even as I have of fertile England's soil.

A day will come when York shall claim his own;
And therefore will I take the Nevils' parts,
And make a show of love to proud Duke Humphrey,
And when I spy advantage, claim the crown,
For that's the golden mark I seek to hit:
Nor shall proud Lancaster usurp my right
Nor hold the sceptre in his childish fist
Nor wear the diadem upon his head,
Whose church-like humour fits not for the crown.
Then, York, be still awhile, till time do serve:
Watch thou and wake, when others be asleep
To pry into the secrets of the State.

This speech explains York's plans and the course of the play, revealing how he intends to double-cross his allies, the Nevils.

Shakespeare thus, by the words that he puts into York's mouth, disintegrates York and exposes his selfish ambitions. However, he represents the Duke of Lancaster in the later play, *Richard II*, as essentially a great patriot by giving him words that the poet never surpassed in expressing his love for England.

Imagine the effect of the staging of the *Henry VI* plays (if that is what they were) for Queen Elizabeth and her court in Whitehall over Christmas 1591–1592. The Queen must have been pleased with her new playwright, someone who spoke so clearly and with such patriotism for England and who gave her predecessors and by implication herself such a glowing tribute. It was the Tudors, the plays projected, who brought stability and order to the English state. Placed before the general public at the Rose some two months later, they attracted large admiring audiences and as propaganda helped to cement the relationship between the sovereign and her subjects.

The Battle of Bosworth (1485) provides the finale for Shakespeare's first tetralogy of history plays. The army led by the Earl of Richmond (Henry Tudor) defeats the forces of Richard III, killing Richard. Boyce commentates:

Shakespeare's presentation of this event is highly elaborate and symbolic. The prelude to the battle, in 5.3, features councils of war and opposing statements of purpose, climaxed by the appearance of the spirits of Richard's victims. This is far more significant to the narrative than the minor vignettes of combat ... The play is then closed by Richmond's coronation, as he proclaims an end to the wars. Historically, this prediction could not have been certain. However, the playwright's purpose was not reportorial but dramatic, almost sacramental: the treachery and violence enacted in the 'Henry VI' plays and *Richard III* are expiated in a ritual letting of blood followed by a formal reconciliation. (p. 71)

Derby

> Courageous Richmond, well hast thou acquit thee!
> Lo! here, in this long-usurped royalty
> From the dead temples of this bloody wretch
> Have I pluck'd off, to grace thy brows withal:
> Wear it, enjoy it, and make much of it.

Richmond

> Great God of heaven, say amen to all!
> But, tell me, is young George Stanley living?

Derby

> He is, my lord, and safe in Leicester town ...

Richmond

> We will unite the white rose and the red;
> Smile, heaven, upon this fair conjunction.
> England has long been mad and scarred herself.
> O, now let Richmond and Elizabeth,
> The true succeeders of each royal house,
> By God's fair ordinance conjoin together;
> And let their heirs—God, if thy will be so—
> Enrich the time to come with smooth-fac'd peace,
> With smiling plenty, and fair prosperous days!

We notice that the two Stanleys, Thomas and William, who really fought at the Battle of Bosworth (although historians are in some doubt about the actual contribution of Sir Thomas) are conflated to one in Shakespeare's play and given a name—Derby—which only one of them acquired shortly afterwards, when Sir Thomas was granted the earldom. This was a rewriting of history. However, Queen Elizabeth would have approved, seeing her grandfather Henry Tudor in triumph, bringing the internecine conflict to an end and proclaiming peace and order in England, which she had so passionately espoused and worked for. The Stanleys would also be very pleased, their ancestors' doubtful conduct on the field of Bosworth deleted by Shakespeare and replaced by a vigorous portrait of allegiance to Henry, with a Stanley ('Derby') on the battlefield triumphantly placing the crown on the head of the first Tudor monarch.

Is it too fanciful to imagine Shakespeare's fine description of Henry Tudor, and the partisan evocation of the Battle of Bosworth, being written in Lancashire, in 1590–1591, featuring Henry Tudor, a descendant of John of Gaunt, step-son to the Derby of the play (shortly to be earled after Bosworth), by a young man determined to make his mark upon English culture, writing an account of part of the colourful history of his Lancashire patrons, the Stanleys?

9

The Stanley Phoenix and the Salusbury Turtle

Any 'collected edition' of the published works of William Shakespeare will in all likelihood include the poem *The Phoenix and the Turtle*. The poem originally had no title. This is distinctive because it would be the only short poem in the collection, apart from any taken from the plays. The other two poems which would be included are *Venus and Adonis* and *The Rape of Lucrece,* long narrative poems.

The Phoenix and the Turtle, however, is quite different. It has no conventional single 'real-life' or invented narrative. It is abstract, dense, spare, and puzzling.

It first appeared in the final pages of a very obscure book called *Love's Martyr*, published in 1601 by London bookseller and publisher Edward Blount in a quarto edition printed by Richard Field. In 1608, Blount registered for publication two of Shakespeare's plays, *Antony and Cleopatra* and *Pericles*, but they never appeared. It is suggested that Shakespeare knew Blount personally. Blount and Isaac Jaggard jointly held the rights to sixteen plays in Shakespeare's First Folio—all but two of those that had not been previously published—making them leading members of the syndicate that financed its printing.

Richard Field (1561–1624), printer of *Love's Martyr*, is also assumed to be a friend of Shakespeare's, hailing from Stratford. Field first published the young playwright's first ambitious literary work *Venus and Adonis*, which was dedicated to the Earl of Southampton. It can be deduced from above particulars that *Love's Martyr* was produced by two of the best people in the book trade in London and that Shakespeare may have had a hand in advising on its publication.

Only two copies of *Love's Martyr's* first impression have survived; one is in the Folger Shakespeare Library in Washington DC, where the present writer has examined it. The main text consists of verses, mostly very amateurish and incoherent, by Robert Chester. This man has been clearly identified by Prof. Duncan-Jones (see p. 103 of *Shakespeare's Poems*) as the Robert Chester who was 'admitted to the Middle Temple in February 1600, retaining lodgings there

Portrait of John Salusbury. This portrait in oils painted *c.* 1592 by an unknown artist was on display in Lleweni, Denbigh. Moses Griffith, itinerant artist, made this copy *c.* 1780, which was printed in colour in a special edition of Pennant's *Tours in Wales*.

until Novemeber 1601. His residence there neatly encompasses the period within which *Love's Martyr* was prepared and published.' John Salusbury had been admitted to the Middle Temple in March 1595, beginning a period of some six years when he spent time in London.

John Salusbury was knighted in June 1601. As Sir John, he had taken his seat as a Member of Parliament by 16 December 1601. This signals that the reputation of the family had recovered, after the alleged treason, and capital punishment, of John's brother, Thomas, who was one of the conspirators in the Babington Plot, which involved killing Queen Elizabeth and enthroning the Catholic Mary.

Love's Martyr is a volume published in praise of John Salusbury. The title asserts his love for his wife Ursula. Four 'modern writers' (Shakespeare, Marston, Chapman, and Jonson) all contribute verses. The last three named write lines of dedication and praise, but Shakespeare's contribution is different, much darker and much more obscure.

If we read *The Phoenix and the Turtle* as allegory and as relating to the real-life story of John Salusbury and his wife Ursula (Stanley), starting with John's grief at the loss of his brother Thomas, we presuppose friendship and familiarity between them and Shakespeare.

A recent account of the poem by Frank Kermode (*Shakespeare's Language*, Penguin, 2000) places it at the pinnacle of Shakespeare's art:

> A remarkable work with no obvious parallel in the canon but one that tells us something about his language and interests at the turn of the century. Here there was no question of the audience being distracted; this work was meant for the page ... The poem surely represents a critical moment in the development of his art and is a key document in any discussion of Shakespeare as poet.

We can ask ourselves: why should a poem that Shakespeare had worked on with such commitment, intellect, and high art be included in a publication in effect published by and dedicated to an obscure nobleman who does not, as far as current orthodoxy allows, feature in the foreground topography of his life? Could it be that Sir John Salusbury and his wife are more important in Shakespeare's life than literary scholars have believed?

The poem's date of composition, according to Kermode, was in or about 1600. It was written when the text of *Love's Martyr* was being prepared for the London printer; it seems that approaches to the other 'modern writers' were made at about the same time. It is notable that these contributors were London-based playwrights and poets. It is this writer's belief (following Honigmann) that when Shakespeare picked up his pen to write a contribution to Chester's manuscript, his mind evoked the circumstances of the funeral of

Thomas Salusbury, John's elder brother, in 1586, some thirteen years earlier, which appears in coded form at the beginning of the poem. I am not saying that Shakespeare was at the funeral, but I believe someone in the Salusbury or Derby families told him of it.

Shakespeare had Catholic sympathies: the capital punishment of Thomas in September 1586 would have stirred deep emotions, but they had to be disguised.

The Salusburys were a prominent family of north-east Wales. They owned lands in the central part of the Vale of Clwyd, 2 miles to the east of the old market town of Denbigh, centred on their ancestral home, the mansion called Lleweni. This word translates as 'place of the lion' in Welsh, reflecting the family emblem, a white lion, which persists to this day on the badge of Denbighshire. The house was, in the main, demolished in 1815–1817, although a central section still remains. In addition to their Clwyd holdings, the family-owned lands in the Conwy Valley and in Anglesey were inherited through the Tudor line.

John Salusbury's mother, Catrin of Berain, was a granddaughter of Sir Roland Velville, alleged to be the first-born son of Henry Tudor by a Breton lady (this royal link is summarily dismissed by Ralph Griffiths and Roger Thomas in their book *The Making of the Tudor Dynasty* as 'nothing more than a myth

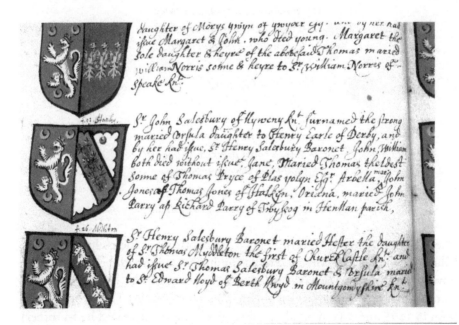

From *The Colour Book,* Denbighshire Archives, Ruthin. Salusbury family crest displaying the white lion of John Salusbury and the three stags' heads, representing Ursula, daughter of Henry, Fourth Earl of Derby, of the Stanley family, joining in marriage in 1586.

inspired by Henry Tudor's early life', p. 175). Henry Tudor, Earl of Richmond, standard-bearer of the Lancastrian cause, fled to Brittany in 1471 to avoid possible capture by the Yorkists. He returned in 1485, though Milford, south-west Wales, with an army which marched, extraordinarily, for fifteen days to the battlefield at Bosworth, near Leicester. Here, Richard III was assassinated and Henry Tudor pronounced himself Henry VII of England.

Catrin of Berain's first husband, John Salusbury, a son of Sir John Salusbury, was buried at Llanefydd in 1566. She was buried in the same place in 1591 (although no trace survives). Thomas, their first son, was executed in London in 1586 for his part in the Babington Plot to kill Queen Elizabeth. The second son, another John Salusbury, was born in the year his father died, 1566, and was therefore about two years younger than William Shakespeare. We do not know where Thomas's funeral took place: Llenefydd and Bodfari are possibilities, as is Whitchurch, the church close to Lleweni where the grandfather was buried.

John Salusbury married Ursula Stanley, natural daughter of Henry, the Fourth Earl of Derby, on 18 December 1586. A masque was performed at Berain on 27 December. The following lines were presented at this occasion (spellings modernised):

> *Dame Venus dear you may rejoice*
> *At your son cupids happy choice*
> *To him as by the Gods assigned*
> *For to delight his doleful mind....*

> *The lion ramping for his prey*
> *A princely bird he did aspie*
> *And having wings to fly at will*
> *Yet caught her fast & holds her still*
> *With her to sport as likes them best*
> *Though lions shout us not to jest*
> *A thing most strange yet it is true*
> *God grant them joy and so adieu.*

The registers of Bodfari parish record the baptisms of the children of John Salusbury and his wife, Ursula. Eleven children were born, three girls and nine boys, of whom seven survived infancy. The first-born was Jane, baptised 10 October 1587. A William (probably named after Ursula's half-brother) was born in 1595 and a Ferdinando (named after Ursula's deceased half-brother) in 1599.

In *Love's Martyr*, there is a plea by the writer, Robert Chester, addressed to the Phoenix (identifiable as Ursula Stanley):

Some deepe-read scholler fam'd for Poetrie,
Whose wit-enchanting verse deserueth fame,
Should sing of thy perfections passing beautie,
And eleuate thy famous worthy name ...

'Famous worthy name' could refer to the Stanleys or to the Salusburys. Who might emerge as this 'deep-read scholar famed for poetry'? Perhaps this was deliberately written to encourage or invite William Shakespeare to pen verses in praise of Ursula and John.

The Phoenix poem begins:

Let the bird of loudest lay
On the sole Arabian tree,
Herald sad and trumpet be:
To whose sound chaste wings obey.

But thou shrieking harbinger,
Foul procurer of the fiend,
Auger of the fever's end,
To this troop come thou not near.

The third, fourth, and fifth stanzas read:

From this session interdict
Every fowl of tyrant wing,
Save the eagle, feather'd king;
Keep the obsequy so strict.

Let the priest in surplice white,
That defunctive music can,
Be the death-divining swan,
Lest the requiem lack his right.

And thou treble-dated crow,
That thy sable gender mak'st
With the breath thou giv'st and tak'st,
'Mongst our mourners shalt thou go.

I suggest that the poem was written against the background of the relationship of John and Ursula, at the early stage of their relationship, although I believe the lines were written some fourteen years later.

John and his family would, in the autumn of 1586, be in mourning for the death of his brother Thomas ('his doleful mind' is part of the 'poesie' at the masque performed—amazingly given a happy occasion—at the John and Ursula wedding celebrations in December). The 'tyrant' is Queen Elizabeth, who in effect put Thomas to death. She is the 'bird of loudest lay'.

'The eagle, feathered king' is Henry, the Fourth Earl of Derby, Ursula's father, head of the Stanley family, whose emblem is the eagle: 'king' because he held the ancient role of King of man. The Stanleys had extensive holdings on the Isle of Man. He, however, is friendly to the Salusburys; he wrote close and supportive letters to his son-in-law. Some other references to tyrants in Shakespeare's work have an Elizabeth-reference sub-text. The poem's beginning symbolically depicts Thomas's funeral, from which those who directly and indirectly put him to death ('Every fowl of tyrant wing') should be kept away. Yet even though he was Master of the Queen's Household, Henry was not included in this 'interdiction' (meaning prohibition or exclusion) because he was friendly to the Salusburys. An 'obsequy' is defined by the *NED* (p. 1,352) as 'Funeral rights or ceremonies; a funeral'. Henry would keep the funeral 'strict' in the sense that he would see its ceremonies properly done, including Catholic rites. Excluded would be the anti-Catholics, including those influenced by the hostile and ruthless Elizabeth and her advisors.

The real meaning of these lines is of course heavily disguised in order to protect the writer and the Salusburys and Derbys from the revenge of the anti-Catholics. 'Thou treble dated Crow' refers, in my view, to Ursula, with her family emblem of three stags heads. The story of the phoenix and the turtle, Ursula and John, does not enter the poem until after the crow reference. 'Sable gender' invokes black and gloomy, and a female mourner, who is Ursula. The 'priest in surplice white' evokes church ritual at the burial of Thomas. The church called 'Whitchurch' on Salusbury land at Lleweni, meaning 'white church'. The Carmelite Order of Friars in the Roman Catholic Church, who wore a white mantle with a brown belt, had a missionary in Denbigh.

The second stanza depicts the opposing forces: those of Elizabeth and her Catholic-hunters/killers. The ugly phrase 'Shrieking harbinger' stands for her (now in her final, eccentric, obsessive, years). 'Foul precurer' has 'foul' as a pun; one meaning being 'unpleasant; disgusting': 'procurer' suggests one who has her bidding done by others. 'Auger of the fever's end' refers to pre-knowledge of Ferdinando' death by poisoning: he died after a fever. These are disguised anti-Elizabeth references. It is interesting that Shakespeare sees Elizabeth as behind the death of Ferdinando. Lord Burleigh could well have had a hand in it because he was concerned about the succession, and Ferdinando would have been a candidate for the next sovereign.

Ursula and John Salusbury are in love. References to 'phoenix' and 'turtle' are scattered throughout *Love's Martyr*, evoking Ursula and John. She is the

HEREAFTER
FOLLOVV DIVERSE
Poeticall Eſſaies on the former Sub-
iect;viz: the *Turtle* and *Phœnix.*

Done by the beſt and chiefeſt of our
moderne writers, with their names ſub-
ſcribed to their particular workes:
neuer before extant.

And (now firſt) conſecrated by them all generally,
to the loue and merite of the true-noble Knight,
Sir Iohn Salisburie.

Dignum laude virum Muſa vetat mori.

MDCI.

A page from the final section of Thomas Chester's volume *Love's Martyr*, published in 1601, the year John Salusbury was knighted. The 'modern writers' include William Shakespeare's poem *The Phoenix and the Turtle*, which was originally untitled.

colourful high-born phoenix, the bird of rebirth, a symbol of new life and renewal. She brought new life and hope to the depressed Salusburys through falling in love with John, the eldest surviving son. He is presented as the turtle-dove, an Elizabethan emblem for constancy in marriage because the dove takes only one mate for life. This is of doubtful veracity when we see evidence of his amours, but it is suitably flattering given the nature and purpose of the publication of *Love's Martyr*, which was to extend and elevate the Salusbury name.

'Leaving no posterity' (l. 59) is consistent with the real-life marriage of Thomas and his wife Margaret, given that they had no male children, and so were not in a position to create 'posterity' from their own bloodline. Some critics have identified the phoenix here with Queen Elizabeth, who used the phoenix design and mythology in her wardrobe. This is to misunderstand Shakespeare's pro-Catholic feelings and the historical context. It is difficult to put aside the fact that Queen Elizabeth had John Salusbury's elder brother put to death, after his conspiring in the Babington Plot. Shakespeare never wrote of her with unstinting praise and never wrote a play about her life; his comments about her were always guarded and heavily coded. She was, in his private thoughts, an unscrupulous, power-hungry tyrant ('shrieking' is an ugly term). The phoenix in Shakespeare's poem has a resonance consistent with the death of Thomas followed by a rebirth in the love between John and Ursula, which triumphed over adversity.

Shakespeare's poem is a mysterious and beautiful lyric, an elegy, and heavily metaphorical. It is a suitable dedication to the love between John and Ursula. Their love arose, like the phoenix, out of the ashes of Thomas's death. The theme of eternal love between human beings is asserted in this poem and continues at the heart of Shakespeare's sonnet sequence. Kermode writes:

> *The Phoenix and the Turtle* offers a paradigm of Shakespeare's obsession with the idea of two-in-one, of doubles, of relation between substance and shadow. The birds are doubled in a mutual flame; they are two, but transcendently single, simple not compounded. Reflections on this scheme may be found everywhere in Shakespeare ... in the very texture of its contemporaries *Hamlet* and *Twelfth Night*. (p. 70)

10

Lancashire Words and Imagery: Clifford Broadbent and the Neglected Work of Frances Keen

Alan Keen's book *The Annotator* contains a list of words (p. 205) headed 'Local Words' followed by 'A list of words used in the vernacular of South Lancashire and also by Shakespeare: barn (child); coil (stir); giglet (wanton); keel (coil); pick-thank (parasite); scuth (whip); slough (skin of a snake).' Another list begins thusly:

> And the following Shakespearian words are also found in Lancashire folk-speech: antic (odd); ban (curse); bodge (repair clumsily); case (skin); gawd (trifle); hugger-mugger (slovenly); jump (agree); latch (take hold of); lob (dullard); padock (toad); pash (to strike); reechy (smoky); shive (slice); sneap (chide); thrum (waste end of warp); whittle (small knife).

The above, especially the first list, seem to show that Shakespeare, as part of his huge vocabulary, used words then peculiar to southern Lancashire. This does not prove that he was in Lancashire, but this material certainly adds to the evidence supporting the argument that he might have lived there. Under the heading 'The Vernacular', Eric Sams writes on page 342 of *Shakespeare's Edmund Ironside*:

> Nor ... is homely English neglected ... All these are vigorous verbs, typical of the Ironside style. There too we find, unusually, the dialectical Northern third person plural indicative in –s treated as a correct and acceptable grammatical form. It is not just the slovenly speech of the country clodhopper Stitch that makes him claim that 'foreheads proves'. The young prince Alfred avers that 'maws devours' ... Such idiosyncrasies are featured as typical and distinctive Shakespeare grammar, with examples including 'clamours poisons' (Err), 'favourites flies' (Ham) 'storms makes' (R3). These oddities are extremely common in the First Folio, where they rather clearly derive from Shakespeare's hand. These grammatical regularities are not in accord with the usual London English of the date. They are provincial, like their author. Shakespeare was accustomed to the Northern mode; for him, the inflection in –s was the current and correct form ...

This observation by the minutely observant Eric Sams shows a form of language derived from the north of England, absorbed and used by Shakespeare at the beginning of his writing career; in this case, 'Northern' refers to a territory well north of Stratford, including Lancashire.

Now we move to material created by the late Clifford Broadbent. He published it in an essay in *Notes and Queries*, in April 1956. Broadbent writes:

> In the belief that scattered through Shakespeare's writings there are references to incidents and places he had himself seen, it is the purpose of this essay to review whatever internal topographical evidence there may be which might tend to link Shakespeare with that part of Lancashire where, it is suggested, he spent some of his youth ... nearly all the most significant passages to be quoted are from his early work, when it might be supposed that his recollections of the district would still be fresh in his mind.
>
> ... The principal features of the landscape at Lea Hall, Rufford and Martholme where Shakespeare is assumed to have lived, are briefly as follows. Lea Hall is set on a small stream near where it joins the north bank of the estuary of the River Ribble, which is here so narrow that the opposite bank is very clearly in view.
>
> Rufford Hall is only about seven miles from this opposite bank, and although immediately to the east-south east there is a high ridge (500 feet); Rufford itself is but 30 feet above sea level ... Martholme lies to the N.E. of Rufford, about 20 miles away, in the foothills of the Pennines ... these foothills can be seen in clear weather from both Lea Hall and Rufford.
>
> The scenery thus differs in two obvious respects from that of Stratford—the sea and the hills—and it is the references to these which we must examine for hints as to Shakespeare's possible knowledge of the district.
>
> ... Shakespeare's use of sea-imagery is extensive and involved ... (but) ... when all generalised references have been excluded there remain some passages where the turn of phrase employed can be seen as pointing to the part of the coast we are interested in.
>
> To start with Lea Hall ... the imagery of Sonnet 106 possibly relates to a tidal estuary:

> *Let this sad interim like the ocean be*
> *Which parts the shore, where two contracted new*
> *Come daily to the banks, that, when they see*
> *Return of love, more blest may be the view.*

> When the actual river-bed is only a small part of the estuary, as with the River Ribble near Lea Hall, the rising tide floods over a much bigger area, and does indeed seem to part the shore. Otherwise the phrase is somewhat strange and

would not readily be recognised as applying to the tide rising in the Thames at London for example. The desire to cross such a stretch of sea is repeated in different circumstances in:

Why, then, I do but dream on sovereignty;
Like one that stands upon a promontory,
And spies a far off shore where I would tread,
Wishing his foot were equal with his eye,
And chides that sea that sunders him from hence,
Saying, hell lade it dry to have his way.

                                            3 Henry VI, III, ii, 134

Shakespeare makes several references to the difficulties of crossing tidal waters when opposed by both wind and tide, which may have been brought home to him by crossing of the Ribble from Lea Hall to Rufford: 'It boots not to resist both wind and tide' (*3 Henry VI*, IV, iii, 59) and 'Sail how thou canst, have wind and tide thy friend' (*3 Henry VI*, III, iii, 59). Particularly interesting is:

Now sways it this way like a mighty sea
Forced by the tide to combat with the wind;
Now sways it that way, like the selfsame sea
Forced to retire by fury of the wind.

                                            3 Henry VI, II, v, 6

… on a flat sea-shore when the sea is rough and there is a strong wind off-shore, the waves after breaking do appear first to hesitate and then to retreat before the wind, and this can be known only to someone who has actually seen it.

   We notice that the above sea images are included in *Henry VI*, his first play to be acted on the London stage. In Sonnet 64, Shakespeare claims to have seen the 'hungry ocean' inundate the land, a frequent occurrence in the Ribble estuary before the present containing banks were built:

> *When I have seen the hungry ocean gain*
> *Advantage on the kingdom of the shore*
> *And the firm soil win of the watery main.*

… Shakespeare appeared to have the west coast in mind when he wrote the following passage, although the scene is set on the Kent coast, looking east: 'The gaudy blabbing and remorseful day/Is crept into the bosom of the sea' (*2 Henry VI*, IV).

Mountains

... [these] seem to be largely conventional and do not seem to be so sharply individual as some of his sea-images. However, even if the mountains themselves do not change much, the light on them does (can we guess this without having seen it?). This is a feature which Shakespeare employs in some of his most beautiful poetry, but he makes as well the important and specific statement of Sonnet 33: 'Full many a glorious morning have I seen/Flatter the mountain-tops with sovereign eye.'

He could not have made such a precise claim had he resided only in Stratford and London, but, of course, the statement would have been true had he lived for any length of time in either Lea Hall, or Rufford, or Martholme. At Rufford he could have seen the sun rise over the ridge to the east: 'But look, the morn, in russet mantle clad,/Walks o'er the dew on yon high eastward hills' (*Hamlet* I, i, 166). The sun also rises over the hills in: 'Night's candles are burnt out, and jocund day/Stands tiptoe on the misty mountain tops' (*Romeo and Juliet* III, v, 9). Sunrise again attracts his eye when it 'Fires the proud tops of the eastern pines' (*Richard II*, III, ii, 42). The pines are frequently, in his imagery, on the tops of mountains.

It is most usual in Shakespeare for the sun to rise over the hills; it commonly sets in the sea, as in *2 Henry VI*, IV, i, 1: 'Even from Hyperion's rising in the east/Until his downfall in the sea.'

Broadbent finishes his essay:

One misses in Shakespeare the careful observations of sea and hills similar to those which by their abundance and accuracy tie him so closely to the countryside. Nevertheless there are in his early work a few sufficiently detailed references which are consistent with the theory that Shakespeare was indeed the youth Shakeshaft living near the Ribble estuary.

Another author, the contemporary Peter Ackroyd, in his *Albion: The Origins of the English Imagination* (p. 225) has made an associated point:

... the sea flows everywhere in his drama ... the cold unruly sea of the Anglo-Saxon imagination is so pervasive in the plays of Shakespeare that it seems to break and dissolve into overwhelming mist and storm. Every play ... includes a reference to the sea; it is employed literally and metaphorically ... his language is permeated by its presence.

If our thesis is correct, that Shakespeare as a youth lived for two years or so on the banks of the Ribble in north-west Lancashire, he would be seeing the sea (the Irish Sea) out of his window and would be visited by it as tides, a few hundred yards away, twice a day. Such proximity would explain the frequency of sea imagery in his work.

Frances Keen (wife of Alan) in 1957 published an essay on a single sheet of paper beginning as follows:

PHOENIX. An inquiry into the poems of Robert Chester's 'Love's Martyr' (1601), and the 'Phoenix' Nest' (1593), in relation to Shakespeare's Sonnets and 'A Lover's Complaint'; arising from the recent discoveries which point to the identity of the Youth of the Sonnets ... and also the Stanley circle, which so influenced the early years of Shakespeare in Lancashire and North Wales. Made in preparation of a greater exposition ...

This, to our purposes, is a remarkable publication. It covers ground that we cover, long before the present author contemplated it. Unfortunately, the 'greater exposition' was never published.

Frances Keen quotes from Chester's writing in *Love's Martyr*: 'That hath to name delightsome Paphos Ile, Ouer the mountain tops to trudge be bold ... Where in a vale like Ciparissus grove, Thou shalt behold a second Phoenix love'. This corresponds, says Keen, to the journey from Lleweni, Denbigh, eastwards over the Clwydian Hills towards Hawarden, where Dorothy, Ursula's sister (loved by John Salusbury), lived. The description of the landscape, writes Keen, 'follows exactly with that of the vale of Lleweni, Salusbury's home among the Welsh mountains, where "true Honors lovely Squire" was to take his bride Ursula Stanley from Hawarden "Where on a high hill he this bird shall meet; And of their Ashes ... shall rise, Another Phoenix her to equalize".' (*Love's Martyr* 12–20).

The 'high hill' is the hill on which Hawarden Castle stands. This is very reminiscent of the imagery of Shakespeare's *The Phoenix and the Turtle*. The 'ashies' relate to the death of Thomas and the ending of his love for his wife Margaret; the bird met on the high hill is Ursula (who lived with her sister at Hawarden Castle, which was built on a hill); and the 'another Phoenix' is Dorothy, Ursula's sister. From the evidence of published poems, we know that John Salusbury was involved with both sisters.

Chester's narrative is more complicated (and crude) than that of Shakespeare's in *The Phoenix and the Turtle* because Chester plainly has two phoenix present on the 'high hill', one of which becomes resident in a very agreeable valley. This is consistent with the situation in reality where both Ursula and Dorothy, daughters of Henry, the 4th Earl, lived in his second home, Hawarden Castle, a residential castle on a mound some six miles west of Chester. One of them, Ursula, married John Salusbury in 1586. The other, Dorothy, engaged in a love affair with John, evoked by the many poems he wrote to her (included in the Carleton Brown volume), which we hold is the central real-life circumstance of 'A Lover's Complaint'.

Frances Keen's 'Vale of Lleweni' reference is in fact the valley of the river Clwyd—'Vale of Clwyd'—in north-east Wales, some 20 miles west of Hawarden. It stretches from 6 miles south of Ruthin, incorporates Denbigh and St Asaph, reaching the sea at Rhyl. Denbigh is located at the centre of this valley, on its western edge. To the east of Denbigh, there are hundreds of acres of fertile flat land that originally belonged to the Salusbury family. The River Clwyd runs through this and close to the remaining buildings of the Salusbury ancestral home, Lleweni, most of the original mansion having been demolished in 1816–7. A range of hills (the Clwydian Range) runs parallel to the valley on the eastern side—a few miles from Lleweni—and it is Frances Keen's opinion that this view is represented in Shakespeare's Sonnet 33. The sun, from Denbigh, rises behind these hills, and the description fits:

> *Full many a glorious morning have I seen*
> *Flatter the mountain tops with sovereign eye,*
> *Kissing with golden face the meadows green,*
> *Gilding pale streams with heav'nly archemy,*

Keen quotes the line from Shakespeare's poem 'A Lover's Complaint':

'The broken bosoms that to me belong ... have emptied all their fountains in my well' (spoken by the Adonis of the poem). These 'broken bosoms' are easily identified with the rounded smooth-topped (breast-like) line of the Clwydian Hills with gaps between them, thus 'broken'. John Salusbury, as the owner of the large Lleweni estate, would have owned these hills.

What Frances Keen did not know was that the principal hill here (overlooking Lleweni) is called 'Moel Famau' and that the latter word is derived from the Latin word for 'with breasts', thus 'mammal': animal with breasts. Growing up in Welsh-speaking Denbigh, John Salusbury would almost certainly have been able to speak the local language and would have known the linguistic connection between 'mammau' and bosoms. Also, we note that the three-winged mansion Lleweni had a lake on the Denbigh side, which featured a fountain, and close by, there was a well.

The central argument in this chapter is that some items of language and some topographical imagery used by Shakespeare can be seen as supporting the proposition that he spent time in Lancashire and in north-east Wales.

11

Hawarden Castle and 'A Lover's Complaint'

The old castle comprises a polygonal court about 45 m across, dominated by a round keep on a motte on the west side ... the keep measures 16.8 m in diameter over ashlar-faced walls 4 m thick ... It is assumed that the keep once had a third storey, but nothing of it now remains.

In 1485 Henry VII gave Hawarden and the Earldom of Derby to Lord Stanley, and the king was twice entertained by him at the castle.

(Glossary of Terms. Motte—A steeply sided flat topped mound, usually mostly man-made.)

Mike Salter, *The Castles of North Wales*, p. 71

The poem 'A Lover's Complaint' was published by Thomas Thorpe in the same volume as Shakespeare's sonnets in 1609. The head title states simply 'A Louers complaint. By William Shake-speare'. It was reprinted in 1640, in John Benson's edition of Shakespeare's poems: *Poems: Written by Wil. Shake-speare. Gent.* Incidentally, this hyphenated form of the poet's name is also used in *Love's Martyr*. Scholars debate whether the poem really was Shakespeare's: some say that part of it was, though our present belief is that it was entirely Shakespeare's. There are forty-seven stanzas in rhyme royal, the form employed by Shakespeare in *The Rape of Lucrece* (registered 9 May 1594); it was probably written in the middle to later years of the 1990s.

It is very possible that the original setting of 'A Lover's Complaint' was Hawarden Castle. This is about 2 miles from the Wales–England border and about 6 miles to the west of Chester. This old castle (from the thirteenth century) comprises a polygonal court about 45 m across, dominated by a round keep on a motte on the west side.

The connection between the Stanley family and north-east Wales began with Sir John Stanley (?1350–1414). Later, Sir John's grandson, Thomas, second Baron Stanley, took possession of the lordships of Hawarden and Moldsdale

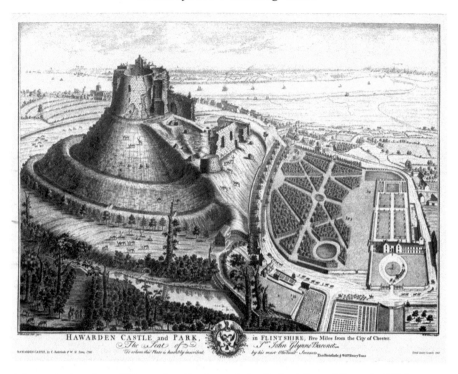

HAWARDEN CASTLE and PARK, in FLINTSHIRE, Five Miles from the City of Chester.

A freestyle drawing of Hawarden Castle made by Badesdale and Toms in 1740.

on his marriage to Eleanor Neville. After Eleanor's death, Thomas married Margaret Beaufort, mother of Henry Tudor, Earl of Richmond. In the period after 1485 and until his death at Lathom in 1504, his estates increased.

The castle was a Stanley retreat and from the 1570s, Henry, the Fourth Earl of Derby, lived here on occasions with Jane Halsall and their children, including the two daughters, Ursula and Dorothy—his 'second family'. Nearby is Broughton, from which this section of the Stanley clan took their name: 'Stanley of Broughton'.

Ferdinando wrote letters citing Hawarden Castle. One, dated March 1581/2, was to Chadderton, Bishop of Chester, says that he and his wife were 'going to dwell at Harden Castle' adding significantly, 'for I am throughe with my father'.

Ten years later, Earl Henry was at Hawarden. Writing to his beloved daughter Ursula Salusbury at Lleweni, he complains that the meeting of 'strangers' to him 'this week' has been so great that he has forborne to send for her, but 'on Tuesday night' means to send his coach for her and 'our little ones' that she may be with him next day, signing himself 'your natural lovinge father' from 'My Castle at Hawarden'. The letter was penned by a scribe but the signature is Henry's.

The first stanza of 'A Lover's Complaint' reads as follows:

From off a hill whose concave womb re-worded
A plainful story from a sistering vale,
My spirits to attend this double voice accorded,
And down I laid to list the sad-tun'd tale;
Ere long espied a fickle maid full pale,
Tearing of papers, breaking rings a-twain,
Storming her world with sorrow's wind and rain.

The details of the hill in the first line are consistent with the topography of the castle on a mound in Hawarden: the motte (some 50 feet high) is topped by a bailey, inside which there is a courtyard with a residential keep. The 'concave' part would be the inside of the keep, which was open to the sky. 'Re-worded' suggests an original story whose details are now being replicated. An explanation of this would be that John Salusbury's love of and marriage to Ursula is repeated now with his love for Dorothy, Ursula's sister. John Salusbury penned many sonnets in praise of Dorothy Halsall; one is printed on page 39 of the Carleton Brown volume with an acrostic formulation of her name in the initial letters of each line.

His infatuation appears to have lasted years, fading away through the time, intermittently, that he spent in London. In 1597, a small volume of his poems was published by Robert Parry of Denbigh, including a number of these love poems, most incorporating acrostics. All the sonnets are Shakespearean in form (with a final couplet).

The second line of 'A Lover's Complaint' contains the clinching word: 'sist'ring'. This, I believe, refers to the two Stanley sisters, Ursula and Dorothy. This would be a most unusual word to use in a poem were it not grounded in original reality, deliberately used as a pointer. In the third line, the 'double voice' can be interpreted as a 'double' love, one for each sister. The poem's narrator (in effect, Shakespeare) lies down in the rural setting to evoke for the reader a sad tale, which is essentially one of complaint by the maid of how she was and is treated by the young male lover, who in reality had married her sister, not her, and who returned later, wishing for favours.

We read of a straw hat, suggesting a rural setting, and a wicker basket ('maund') from which she draws 'a thousand favours ... of amber, crystal and of beaded jet', suggesting that her lover was a man of means; she throws them, disgustedly, in a river. This river could well be the River Dee, which now flows about a mile to the north-east of the castle, but which four centuries ago flowed much closer. She shows her dissatisfaction with her lover by throwing his gifts away. She also has 'folded schedules', which she throws away; these could be papers on which poems were written. The fact that they are folded suggests having been carried in a pocket or bag, and carried on horseback. She also throws away rings. She recovers letters 'With sleided silk feat and affectedly/Enswath'd, ...', which could point to silk used to bind legal papers;

John Salusbury became a Member of the Inns of Court in 1595. As she is thus expressing her disgust, nearby is the following:

> *A reverend man that graz'd his cattle nigh,*
> *Sometime a blusterer, that the ruffle knew*
> *Of court, of city, ...*
> *'Father', she says, 'though in me you behold*
> *The injury of many a blasting hour*

This father could be Henry, the Fourth Earl of Derby, who spent time at the court of Elizabeth, one of the court who came to judgement on the fate of Mary Queen of Scots. A famous illustration of this group shows them wearing ruffles. This word could here be ambiguous; it can also be read as meaning activity, being busy. Henry spent some of his relaxing hours with his second family at Hawarden Castle, away from his London home and his homes in Lancashire, Lathom, New Park (near Ormskirk), and, further to the south, Knowsley (now in Merseyside). That he 'graz'd his cattle' here points to this farming location belonging to him, which is true of Henry and Hawarden Castle.

The young man has many charms. 'Too early I attended/A youthful suit,' she complains, with one 'by nature's outwards so commended,/That maidens' eyes stuck over all his face/Love lacked a dwelling and made him her place'. At the time, Dorothy had no love of her own, so she placed her love with her sister's husband, an attractive young man. He has distinctive hair: 'His browny locks did hang in crooked curls,/And every light occasion of the wind/Upon his lips their silken parcels hurls.' We notice that in Chester's poem in *Love's Martyr*, the 'lovely Squire' of Lleweni (John Salusbury) is described: 'His haire is curl'd by nature mild and meek, Hangs carelesse down to shroud a blushing cheek', thus identifying the hair as soft and light-textured. The portrait of John Salusbury that hung in Lleweni and was copied by itinerant artist Moses Griffith (1747–1819) in *c.* 1778 does indeed show long, light-textured, wavy, brown hair.

He is a young man, he has 'phoenix down' on his chin: this suggests quite a young man. The writer uses the adjective 'beauteous', which Shakespeare was the first to use: it occurs again in Sonnet 41 and in both instances, John Salusbury is the likely subject. He was also very agile and very physical. He was an excellent horse rider. He was quick to take offence: 'if men moved him, he was such a storm', which is how John Salusbury's temperament was (he was involved in a number of fights and physical exchanges). 'He had the dialect and different skill.' Could this refer to his being able to speak Welsh? The N. E. D. (p. 500) defines the word 'dialect' as used in 1579 as 'Manner of speaking, language, speech; esp one peculiar to an individual.'

The young man is a deceiver: 'this man's untrue,/And knew the patterns of his foul beguiling/Heard where his plants in others' orchards grew.' As a matter of fact, John is the acknowledged father of an illegitimate son. 'Plant' incidentally is the Welsh word for children. The young man deceived her by giving her 'fair gems', which he had received from other women. He also gave her his writings: 'Take all these similies'. He had received 'deep-brained sonnets' from his lovers and he seemed to have recycled them by directing them at her (a system that Shakespeare himself used through his sonnets).

We have earlier referred to the 'broken bosoms that to me belong' (line 255) (this section is spoken by the male lover), which is identifiable with the Clwydian Hills owned by the Salusbury Lleweni estate. Professor Melville Richards of Bangor was of the opinion that the name Moel Fammau for the tallest hill in the range was derived from the Latin 'mamma', breast. The same stanza continues: 'I strong o'er them, and you o'er me being strong' (line 257), which associates with John Salusbury, also known as 'John the Strong' because of his physical strength, which he used in his pastime as a wrestler.

The line, 'My parts had power to charm a sacred nun' turns the narrative, spoken by John, apparently to the legend of Catholic Saint Winifred of Holywell, who was raped then beheaded, her head rolling down a hill; where her blood seeped in to the ground at the base, a sacred well was formed. (S. 153–4) In the poem, the male lover dismounts from his horse; he has 'watery eyes … each cheek a river running from a fount/With brinish current downward flowed apace./Oh! How the channel to the stream gave grace;/Who glaz'd with crystal gate the glowing roses/That flame through water which their hue encloses.' (ALC, 286–7) The brine and blood imagery belongs to both stories, the liquid running downwards, and the 'glowing roses' convincingly describes a red colour underwater. This red is consistent with observations made at St Winifred's Well, Holywell, a few miles from Hawarden. The Welsh bard Tudur Aled of Llansannan (*c.* 1405–*c.* 1525) wrote, translated from the original Welsh:

> *In the earth, red-marked stones,*
> *Musk and balm within the world,*
> *A pure white stone with a pure place,*
> *Stones marked with the blood of a white neck.*

Dr Johnson visited the well in 1774. He noted:

> The spring called Winifred's Well is very clear, and so copious that it yields on hundred tuns of water a minute … the well is covered by a lofty circular arch supported by pillars, and over this arch is an old Chapel … We then saw a brass work where the lapis Calaminaris is gathered, broken, washed from the earth.

Calaminaris is calamine, an ore of zinc; this oxidises, turning a red colour, commonly called zincite. This could be the explanation for the red colour observed on the stones in the well. He went on:

> Left nothing but the stone at the bottom of the water which bears any mark of ancient superstition and is spotted with red in two or three places, and the Roman Catholics believe from their hearts that it was stained by the blood of their favourite Virgin martyr.
>
> *Dr Johnson & Mrs Thrale's Tour in North Wales, 1774,*
> Bristow, Bridge Books, p. 105

As noted previously, Shakespeare's father named Saint Winifred (of Holywell) as his patron saint. If his son handwrote this in to his 'spiritual will', the particular detail of the red coloured stone would seem to support the proposition that Shakespeare had visited the spot.

Catholic, Tudor and Stanley associations with this Well are reinforced by the fact that Henry Tudor's mother, Margaret Beaufort, second wife to Sir Thomas Stanley, of Bosworth fame, commissioned the chapel part of the shrine in 1490. Father Gerard, one of the few men to escape from the Tower of London, bathed in the well on 3 November 1593. The well is still a popular place of pilgrimage and healing; it has between 30,000 and 40,000 visitors a year.

The fact that 'A Lover's Complaint' was included in the same 1609 volume as Shakespeare's sonnets by publisher Thomas Thorpe has puzzled many commentators. There is a possible link between them: that of his wife's sister, the 'another phoenix'.

It is possible to postulate an intrinsic linking of the two texts: that both contain (among other stories) the same story—of two triangles that involve the same people, a woman and two men. It is clear from 'A Lover's Complaint' that the narrator/writer is Shakespeare. If the account placed before the reader in this chapter is correct, then the complaining woman is Dorothy Halsall and her Adonis (adept horseman and landowner) is John Salusbury, with the other male being Shakespeare.

In his excellent edition *The Sonnets and A Lover's Complaint* (Penguin Books, 1986), John Kerrigan writes:

> The turn the tradition took in 1594 with the publication of *Willobie His Avisa* ... This may describe a triangular situation, with something of the dark comedy we find in the Sonnets—a triangle refracted in 'A Lover's Complaint'—but, again, the anxiety of the poet in Shakespeare's collection is quite different from that of W. S. in *Willobie*. (p. 392)

My suggestion is that Shakespeare's sonnets contains the same triangular relationship, encapsulated in Sonnets 40, 41, and 42. The strongly sexual nature of the relationship with the dark lady of the later sonnets is quite unlike the earlier relationship with the woman in sonnet 42: 'That thou hast her, it is not all my grief,/And yet it may be said I loved her dearly' and therefore I see them as different people.

A full and believable explanation of the above and the 'correct' identification of the pronouns 'thou' and 'her' remains for another time. I would now suggest that the 'thou' could point to John Salusbury of Denbigh: strong man, deceiver, lover, flatterer, pursuer of his wife's sister, possessor of the 'lascivious grace' of Shakespeare's Sonnet 40; and that the 'her' could be Dorothy, his wife's sister and 'another phoenix'.

'That thou hast her,' seems to be a felt comment by Shakespeare, who had love for Dorothy, but who had to step aside in obeisance because John Salusbury was pursuing her.

I propose that John Salusbury was one of the young men featured in Shakespeare's sonnets, and that he was the lusty young man who was subject to much complaint in 'A Lover's Complaint'.

The inclusion of 'A Lover's Complaint' in the same volume as Shakespeare's sonnets, is, I suggest, not random and unconnected. Both works are linked thematically and geographically. Both identify a woman who was courted by Shakespeare's friend; a woman with whom Shakespeare himself was also involved with, ('I loved her dearly,' he writes in Sonnet 42) and whom he later lost. 'Take all my loves, my love' he says in Sonnet 40, addressing John Salusbury as 'my love'. Dorothy Halsall must have been an attractive, independently-minded woman, and possibly fair-haired.

It is possible that the manuscript of Shakespeare's sonnets and the poem 'A Lover's Complaint' was possessed by John Salusbury in London, because he appears in both, and that it was he who passed the material to publisher Thorpe.

12

A Possible Young Man of
the Sonnets

From the Earl of Southampton to Sir John Salusbury to 'Mr. W. H.' to Frances Manners, Earl of Rutland, Shakespeare's visible patrons were all male.

Ungentle Shakespeare, Katherine Duncan-Jones, p. 130

Shakespeare's sonnets are a major part of his published work and a source of much pleasure for readers and raw material for literary critics and biographers. They all stand on their own, but a real-life experience is felt by readers and scholars to lie behind their composition. They are described in terms of 'a biography of the soul' and although Shakespeare took care to exclude all empirical references to real-life people and places, an unmarried young man is clearly the subject of the early set, which consist of a plea for a beautiful high-born man to marry and have children.

Received wisdom has it that the one 'inspirer' of all these sonnets was the Earl of Southampton. Shakespeare in the early 1590s dedicated two long poems to him, in an attempt to attract patronage. It is possible that the early series of sonnets in the 'beget' mode was presented by Shakespeare in an attempt (perhaps 'nudged' by Burleigh and his court acquaintances) to persuade the rich and well-connected Earl to marry Elizabeth de Vere, daughter of the Earl of Oxford.

The term *roman à clef* (a novel introducing real characters under fictitious names) has particular relevance here in our consideration of the biographical and literary inspiration for these sonnets. Although they are not of course a novel, they do have a narrative, albeit irregular: the reader does sense that particular real-life experience lies behind their creation. An error we can easily fall into is assuming that only one relationship applies in the main body of the work. My feeling is that the sonnets feature, anonymously, a minimum of three relationships between the author and three young men, and two relationships

Henry Wriothsley, 3rd Earl of Southampton (1573–1624) (1594).

between the author and two women, one in the early sonnets centred on Sonnet 40 and the other, with the 'woman coloured ill' of Sonnet 144.

Another error is to assume that the sonnets in their present printed order were written in that order, chronologically. On the contrary, it is entirely likely that Shakespeare wrote his sonnets over a period of many years and that when it came to publication, he passed them to the printer in their new order, after some of them had been 'recycled'. We need to consider 'doubleness', writing that can apply to more than one person. In his search for patronage, he could write a number of sonnets inspired by one nobleman, show them to him, and later in life show the same poems to another nobleman, in another search of new patronage. This would be typical of his habit of economy with his texts.

Few commentators on this early set of sonnets have drawn attention to Shakespeare's striking comment in sonnet 10: 'For thou art so possessed with murd'rous hate,/That 'gainst thyself thou stick'st not to conspire,' and asked themselves if this is consistent with what we know of the very young Earl of Southampton. Did he have any good reason for hate? Apparently not; he grew up in privileged and settled circumstances. This could apply to Ferdinando, who was the subject of some very murky events in the Catholic Elizabeth I offensive. Another who had good reason to be 'possessed with murd'rous hate' was John Salusbury of Denbigh. His brother, Thomas, had been implicated in the Babington Plot and had been put to death at Tyburn, London, in September 1586. We have presented a scenario in which Shakespeare evokes Thomas's funeral, in *The Phoenix and the Turtle*. The ''gainst thyself' suggests that a suppression of anger would be tactful, which fits the circumstances of John Salusbury's life, when revenge against Elizabeth and her courtiers, who put his brother to death by a most barbarous method, would be counterproductive in relation to the process of recovering his family's name at court, which came to a head when Elizabeth knighted him in 1601 and he became a Member of Parliament for Denbighshire at the end of the year.

Katherine Duncan-Jones, in her volume *Shakespeare's Poems* (with H. R. Woudhuysen, 2007) has brought to the fore much interesting and pertinent information on *Love's Martyr* and John Salusbury. She writes in her introduction:

> Unlike other modern editors, we have attempted to situate *Love's Martyr* within the career of its dedicatee, the courtier-poet Sir John Salusbury. We believe that Shakespeare was aware of other volumes of verse dedicated to Salusbury, and that he may even have been acquainted with the man himself. (p. 3)

This comment must refer to the Parry volume, the subject of much of the following discussion.

In the sonnets, we have references to the male love-subject's poetry-writing: 'So is it not with me as with that muse,/Stirred by a painted beauty to his verse' (Sonnet 21). His poems are in a book: the 'tables' of Sonnet 122: 'Thy gift, thy tables, are within my brain/Full charactered with lasting memory'. Sonnet 32 has, 'Had my friend's muse grown with this growing age,/ ... and poets ... /Theirs for their style I'll read, his for his love.' Shakespeare's Sonnet 77 compares his friend's writings to his own, ending 'and much enrich thy book', referring to a book of his friend's writing. He implores his friend to write his experiences rather than try to keep them in memory: 'Commit to these waste blanks,' he says, meaning to write on paper, which is worthless without his friend's writing.

Did Southampton write poetry and have a book of his verse published? Not as far as we know. This limits the field of our three males to Ferdinando, Fifth Earl of Derby (before his death in the spring of 1594), and John Salusbury. The Earl's work was published in a popular anthology, *Belvedere* (1600), but it was not published in a single volume entirely of his own writings.

A small volume of John Salusbury's poems was published in 1597. This was sponsored and published by Robert Parry, of Denbigh, under the puzzling title *Sinetes Passions*. The only sense I can make of this is to suggest that it means 'sinful passions' (given John Salusbury's waywardness in love). The title continues, 'Offered for an incense at the shrine of the Ladies which guided his distempered thoughts. The patrons patheticall Posies, Sonnets, Madrigals, Roundelays'.

It is clear that John Salusbury did not behave in a manner towards the opposite sex that we might consider respectful and conventional. He had a number of lovers, including Dorothy Halsall and Helena Owen. This collection of his writings begins with thirteen poems headed 'Posie'; they are very abstract and allusive. They are followed by a collection of thirty-one sonnets (headed 'Sonetto'). A number of these poems spell out the names Dorothy Halsal [sic] and Helena Owen acrostically. Dorothy was John Salusbury's wife's sister, from Henry, the Fourth Earl of Derby's 'second family' living at Hawarden Castle.

John Salusbury's Sonnet 26 contains the following lines:

> *That which this day, could finest wittes allure;*
> *To-morrowe, CORIDON doth cast away,*
> *The Iron being hot who list for not to strike,*
> *Shall sure, being cold, neu'r forge it to his mind,*
> *And all those partes, moueth louve to like;*
> *Eu'n so in time daunger attends delaye,*
> *For time and tide for no mans pleasures stay.*

This poem reads as a statement of regret at his friend's leaving, saying, however, that his departure is necessary, otherwise he would be in 'danger'. Why should he be in danger? This suggests danger from the Catholic hunters, who may discover Shakespeare's whereabouts. CORIDON has Shakespearean (shepherd-like) overtones—he uses it in *A Midsummer Night's Dream*; the imagery of the striking iron links with a shaken iron spear; and the danger would be real if Shakespeare was hiding in Lleweni, Denbigh, John Salusbury's home, in fear of the unscrupulous Catholic hunters and their deathly judgments.

The last selection of John Salusbury's verse in the Robert Parry volume consists of six poems, two headed 'MADDRIGALL' and two headed 'ROUNDE-DELAY'. A short six-line poem describes a person asleep in bed in the morning; the person has a 'soft-sweete cheeke on pillow soft reposing; … Then sayde were I that pillowe, Deere for thy loue I would not weare the willowe'. The word 'sweet' is a very Shakespearean word. The fact that the gender of the sleeper is not revealed is perhaps significant.

This Parry volume contains fifty poems by John Salusbury, so his creation of verse was not just occasional and slight. He could be called 'a poet'. It does seem that he wrote few poems after 1597; this fits in with Shakespeare's statement that his friend's muse did not 'grow with this growing age'.

There is an intriguing reference to 'deep brained sonnets' in line 209 of Shakespeare's long poem 'A Lover's Complaint'. The writing of sonnets was something John Salusbury did, which may be an identifying link.

A drawing of Lleweni, Denbigh, from the mid-eighteenth century, showing the tall trees.

Turning to Shakespeare's Sonnet 33, Frances Keen has identified the view in the first lines as the view from Lleweni, Denbigh, the home of the Salusburys, eastwards, towards the Clwydian Hills, with the morning sun rising behind the hills.

The topography here has hills to the east and in the foreground fields and streams; clearly a pleasing rural location. It has no similarity with the topography of Stratford or of Titchfield (the home of the Earl of Southampton). It has much similarity to the setting of Lleweni, in its rich parkland, with the River Clwyd close.

'Doubleness' fascinated Shakespeare. His plays are full of double or multiple identities: males dressed as females and the opposite. It may well stand for his sexual orientation. That certain accounts, writings, and descriptions could apply to more than one place or person is consistent with his writing and lifestyle. We could call it 'multiple use', a technique designed to flatter a patron or prospective patron, the same writing having been used to engage an earlier, different, person.

The point is well made in Stephen Greenblatt's fine book, *Will in the World*:

> Could Shakespeare have, as some scholars have proposed, been addressing both young men in succession, cleverly recycling the love tokens? Could some of those same love tokens have originated as poems addressed to other young men or women whom the poet was wooing?

In Shakespere's sonnets, after the first group, (*c.* 1–26) there is a distinct change of subject. Talk of beauty, marriage and procreation, much of it abstract, ceases and allusions become more actual; there is talk of travelling, distance, the weather (especially clouds), and some personal 'disgrace'.

The first group relates to marriage and procreation, followed by sonnets which are redolent of a visit and further visits to a young man's home by Shakespeare, who actually had travelling players and plays in distant towns to attend to. He complains of lack of sleep and of weariness brought on by travel. The rural site of the young man's home seems some distance away from Shakespeare's usual haunts ('How far I toil').

See Sonnet 28:

> *How can I then return in happy plight*
> *That I am debarred the benefit of rest—*
> *When day's oppression is not eased by night, ...*
> *The one by toil, the other to complain*
> *How far I toil, still further off from thee.*
> *I tell the day to please him thou art bright,*
> *And dost him grace when clouds do blot the heaven ...*

See also Sonnet 29:

> *When in disgrace with fortune and men's eyes,*
> *I alone beweep my outcast state ...*
> *And look upon myself and curse my fate,*
> *Wishing to me like to one more rich in hope,*
> *Featured like him, like him with friends possessed ...*
> *Haply I think on thee, and then my state,*
> *Like to the lark at break of day arising,*
> *From sullen earth....*

What was this 'disgrace'? No commentator is sure about this. It is possible that it is as a result of charges of plagiarism; or it could relate to his father's Catholicism and financial failure; or it could be the 'disgrace' of being a mere player (similar to being a vagabond in public reputation). 'Lark ... break of day ...[and] sullen earth' refer to the traveller's condition. The admired young man is clearly of much higher social standing, and more attractive physically, than Shakespeare, who feels inferior.

The following is from Sonnet 33:

> *And from the forlorn world his visage hide,*
> *Stealing unseen to west with this disgrace.*
> *Ev'n so my sun one early morn did shine*
> *With all triumphant splendour on my brow;*
> *But out alack, he was but one hour mine,*
> *The region cloud hath masked him from me now ...*

The 'friend' is to the west, in another region. Shakespeare is to the east of him, travelling, working. He travels ('unseen' implies secrecy and separation) to the west to be with his friend. There, he sees the sun rising from his friend's house, in a rural place with streams, and hills to the east ('the meadows green,/ ... pale streams'). However, he was only with his friend one hour. The clouds act as a symbolic barrier between the two.

There is a realism in this group of sonnets, a sense of actual journeys, of a real person and location. There is a sense of regret at his own work and position in life. It is consistent with the writer's working as a travelling actor for the Stanleys and the Chamberlain's Men, riding westwards to Denbigh, and returning.

Sonnet 19 has: 'Devouring time, blunt thou the lion's paw'. Parry uses the same 'Deuouring [*sic*] time' in his poem in praise of John Salusbury: had Shakespeare read Parry, or *vice versa*? The reference to 'the lion's paw' seems self-conscious and pointed; it may identify the young man. The white lion was the heraldic emblem of the Salusbury family and their mansion Lleweni was named after it: 'llew' in Welsh means lion; 'wen' means white. Blunting the paw of the lion would symbolise a taming (through time) of the impulsive, vigorous nature of the lion-person.

The fourth line of this sonnet reads, 'And burn the long-lived phoenix in her blood'. The phoenix here is female. If the 'lion's paw' recalls John, this phoenix recalls the high-born Ursula, his wife after December 1586. Traditionally in England, a bird is a symbol of a long and successful marriage. This uses similar imagery to that in Chester's *Love's Martyr* and Shakespeare's *The Phoenix and the Turtle*. In both, the phoenix is a representation of new life, following a catastrophe, of singleness in union.

See Sonnet 36: 'Let me confess that we two must be twain,/Although our undivided loves are one.' This echoes the one-as-two/two-as-one theme of the poem, particularly its lines 25–26, 'So they lov'd, as love in twain/Had the essence but in one'.

Lines in Sonnet 36 read:

> *I may not evermore acknowledge thee,*
> *Lest my bewailed guilt should do thee shame;*
> *Nor thou with public kindness honour me,*
> *Unless thou take that honour from thy name*

At this point, an echo of a significant identificatory phrase from Chester's *Love's Martyr* emerges: 'His name is Liberall honor …' This is in the following verses (The Carleton Brown volume, introduction p. lxvi):

> *Hard by a running stream or crystall fountaine,*
> *Wherein rich Orient pearle is often found,*
> *Enuiron'd with a high and steepie mountain,*
> *A fertill soile and fruitful plot of ground,*
> *There shall thou find true Honors louely Squire,*
> *That for this Phoenix keepes Promethus fire.*
>
> *His bower wherein he lodgeth all the night,*
> *Is fram'd of Cedars and high loftie Pine,*
> *I made his house to chastice thence despight,*
> *And fram'd it like this heauenly roofe of mine:*
> *His name is Liberall honor, and his hart,*
> *Aymes at true faithfull seruice and desart*

We notice how the topography of the above description appears to match that of Sonnet 33, with streams and fertile land in the foreground and hills nearby to the east. This country house appears to be surrounded by tall cedar and pine trees. When Dr Johnson visited Lleweni, Denbigh, on 29 July 1774, with his friend Mrs Thrale, who was the last survivor of the original Salusbury family, he wrote in his diary:

> In the lawn of Lleweney [*sic*] is a spring of fine water which rises above the surface into a stone basin, from which it runs to waste in a continual stream through a pipe. There are very large trees ... The ground is beautifully embellished with woods, and diversed by inequalities. The hall at Llewenny is 40 feet long and 28 broad. The Gallery 120 feet long (all paced); the Library 42 feet long, and 28 broad. The dining parlour 30 feet long 26 broad.

In a note dated 17 August, Dr Johnson writes:

> Adiew, Llewenny! I do not often delight much with people or with places, but Llewenny is a place, and Mrs Cotton a person, that I like extremely, and with whom I lived quite at my ease, and very much to my liking ...

Carleton Brown writes (p. lxvi, introduction):

> Several points in these lines suggest that the subject of this description is Sir John Salusbury. In the first place the landscape agrees with that of Lleweni, which was situated in the fertile meadows bordering the river Clwyd and environed by hills and mountains. Again in the phrase 'louely Squire' Chester uses a term which was descriptive of Salusbury's rank until he was knighted in June 1601—and there can be no doubt that *Love's Martyr* was composed before this date ... Finally, it is to be noted that these stanzas in *Love's Martyr* not only give a picture of the Turtle-dove but also give him a name: 'His name is Liberall honor.' Here, if anywhere, one feels, a definite clue to his identity must be intended. In his poems in the Christ Church MS. Chester has shown a fondness for acrostics; may it not be that here he resorted to an anagram? Out of 'Liberall honor' I can make nothing, but if one take instead the Latin equivalent, *Honos liberalis*, the letters will be found to spell IOHON SALLSBERI. If this be accidental, it is at least a curious coincidence. The spelling 'Sallsberi', it may be granted, does not occur elsewhere ... (but) when the laxity of Elizabethan spelling is considered exactness cannot be insisted upon ...

All the aforesaid supports a contention that John Salusbury, squire of Lleweni, Denbigh, great-great-grandson of Henry VII and cousin to Queen Elizabeth, could well have been an original (not 'the original') of the 'beauteous' young man of the sonnets. Shakespeare is seen as exercising a process of conflation or interleaving in this long series of sonnets whereby two or three, or perhaps more, original and similar real young men are featured. A significant lack of detail in the text—which would identify an original subject, with reference to physical appearance and to location and landscape—is characteristic of Shakespeare's sonnets, concealing the real-life original person and setting of a particular sonnet, enabling more than one young man to believe that the sonnet was inspired by and written for him.

John Salusbury was born late in 1566, which makes him some two-and-a-half years younger than William Shakespeare. The early sonnets urge a young man to marry and have children. This is consistent with the situation in the second half of 1586 when John succeeded to the Salusbury fortune after his brother was executed for treason in September. This traumatic event would explain the 'music sadly' of Sonnet 8 and the 'possessed with murd'rous hate' (against the killers of his brother) of Sonnet 10. I believe that 'doubleness' applies, that Southampton and Salusbury are the 'inspirers' here.

Sonnet 3's 'Thou art thy mother's glass, and she in thee/Calls back the lovely April of her prime' could refer Southampton's mother, but also to John's mother, the celebrated and beautiful Catrin of Berain (1535–1591). She married four of North Wales's wealthiest and most influential men. Portraits of her and of her son John hung in Lleweni when Dr Samuel Johnson visited in the 1770s, and they very likely hung there in the 1590s. The portrait of John was copied by itinerant painter Moses Griffith in the 1770s and included in an edition of Thomas Pennant's *Tour of Wales*.

Shakespeare's sonnets contain a number of references to his friend in a painting:

> *So is it not with me as with that muse,*
> *Stirred by a painted beauty to his verse..* (21)

> *Mine eye hath played the painter and hath stelled*
> *Thy beauty's form in table of my heart..* (24)

> *With my love's picture then my eye doth feast,*
> *And to the painted banquet bids my heart ...*
> *So either by thy picture or my love,*
> *Thyself away are present still with me ...*
> *thy picture in my sight.* (47)

If Shakespeare was employed by Henry, the Fourth Earl of Derby, in 1586, as we have postulated, there was a very good reason why Shakespeare would urge John, the new Squire of Lleweni, to marry and have children shortly after the death of his brother in September 1586. It is possible that some of the early sonnets were written later and 'folded in to' the 'beget' sonnets already written to Southampton. A son of John and his high-born Stanley bride would inherit the Salusbury wealth rather than have it go to his mother's fourth husband, Edward Thelwall, and his descendants (John's mother, Catherine of Berain died in August 1591, at the age of fifty-six.). A 'recycling' of praise-sonnets by Shakespeare from those directed first for the Earl of Southampton and secondly for John Salusbury some four or five years later (in the early 1590s, when he wanted his patronage) is entirely possible. This 'multi-purpose' method, in its ingenuity of purpose and economy, is understandable in the context of Shakespeare's approach to securing patronage. I believe that the composition of the sonnets was sporadic and covered a much longer time period than some commentators have allowed. It may be that he continued to write new sonnets, to join the existing ones and revise existing ones, until the announcement made in Stationers' Register of 20 May 1609 that Thomas Thorpe intended to publish 'SHAKESPEARES SONNETS'.

Katherine Duncan-Jones writes:

> Unlike every other Elizabethan sequence, Shakespeare's sonnets 1–126 celebrate a young male love-object; and so in a sense does *A Lover's Complaint*, much of which consists of a nameless maiden's anatomy of irresistible charms and wiles of her young seducer. In making a young man's beauty and worth his central focus, Shakespeare may be seen as overturning the conventions of more than two hundred years of 'Petrarchanism' ...

Shakespeare's Sonnets, p. 47

Henry's 'natural' daughter Ursula would make a very good marriage with the wealthy, young man John Salusbury, who, in a parallel situation to the Stanley family, was a relative of Henry VII, just as Ursula's half-brother Ferdinando was. Not only would this marriage bring additional wealth, power, and influence to both sides, it also worked geographically, by adding to the Stanley holdings in north-east Wales a section of the Salusbury holdings westwards, including (in Lleweni) over a thousand acres of the best land in Wales in the centre of the fertile Vale of Clwyd; holdings in the Berain area (west of St Asaph) and property and land centred on Penymynydd in Anglesey, the original home of the Tudors, which Catherine had inherited.

The theory presented above—that John Salusbury was a young man of the sonnets, not the young man—has been supported by a number of propositions: viz. 1. that he had good reason to be angry; 2. that he wrote poetry which was published in a bound volume; 3. that he was high-born and lived in an attractive rural location to the west; 4. that this location had streams and fertile land to the foreground with hills nearby to the east; 5. that he might be identified by the 'lion's paw' and 'phoenix' references; and 6. that he might be identified through the 'honour from thy name' allusion in Sonnet 36, as explained by Carleton Brown in his introduction to his edition of the poems of John Salusbury.

Catherine Duncan-Jones suggests that the same 'fair youth' appears in both the sonnets and 'A Lover's Complaint':

> However, the youth himself constitutes one of the strongest thematic links between 'A Lover's Complaint' and the sonnets. Apparently a wealthy and promiscuous young courtier, he seems to be universally admired and sought after as the fair youth of sonnets 1–126.

The above chapter supports what could be a closer relationship between Shakespeare and John Salusbury than might earlier have been proposed, and that a number of poems—the sonnets, 'A Lover's Complaint', and the Parry poems of John Salusbury—have common interconnected themes and persons. It is proposed that the Halsall sisters, Ursula and Dorothy, play a central part, with Shakespeare and John Salusbury amorously connected with them and with one another.

A Midsummer Night's Dream

The 'Dream' appears purpose-built to suit the subject and occasion, which—
as in Love's Labour's Lost, also evidently designed in the first place to be acted
in private before noble patrons ...

Harold F. Brooks, *A Midsummer Night's Dream, Arden Edition*, 1979:
introduction p. liv

The diary of Robert Parry, son of Harry ap Robert of Tywysog, Henllan, Denbigh, was published in *Archaeologia Cambrensis*, in April 1915. The period covered is from the beginning of Queen Elizabeth's reign to the year 1613.

For 1593, Parry writes (spellings modernised): 'This was a year of great sickness in London so that myself being at the Court of Windsor upon a Sunday, the Bill that week'. Then: '1594. Ao 36 Eliz. The 6th of March being Wednesday ... The 16 of April Ferdinando Earl of Derby deceased as some think by an untimely death but the matter nev' enquired after.... The 25 of April fell such a tempest of rain lightning and hail in this county of Denbigh town so that it carried away the hides and skins of tanners and glovers from the tanningpits and did other great losses'. A later entry reads: 'Ao 39 Eliz 1597 ... [after an entry for 24 September] Will Earl of Derby & his Countesse came to Lleweni and were very royally entertained'.

William was the brother who inherited the earldom after the death of Ferdinando. They were living in the family's two houses in Lancashire: Knowsley and Lathom. Setting out from Knowsley for Denbigh, they would travel about 40 miles. They may have divided the journey by staying at their property Hawarden Castle, which is at about the mid-point.

William Stanley was born in 1561, younger son of the Fourth Earl, Henry, whose heir was Ferdinando, Lord Strange. Like him, William went to St John's College, Oxford, in 1572; and in 1582 at the age of twenty-one, he began his travels in France in the charge of a Welsh tutor, Richard Lloyd. It is conjectured

The title page of the first edition of *A Midsummer Night's Dream*, published by Thomas Fisher in 1600.

that William was in Navarre between 1582 and 1587. Stanley and his tutor Lloyd were back in England and at Lathom, the great Stanley mansion, in June 1587. Before and after this date, he was travelling in Europe, and there are many colourful tales of his exploits, mostly invented or exaggerated. A story set on the Nile in Egypt has him killing a tiger with his sword; another has him in jail for 'blasphemy against the religion of Mahommed' and due to be executed, but a lady intervenes and he is freed. He returned to England to hear that all the estates of the earldom had been settled upon his brother's daughters. The dowager Alice hung onto her and her daughters' assets as long as possible. Alice and William endured seven years of litigation before he successfully recovered most of his family's holdings, which included 'all the houses, lands, castles and appurtenances in Lancashire, Cumberlands, Yorkshire, Cheshire, and many in Wales ... with the old seat in Cannon Row, Westminster (afterwards called Derby Court)'. Anne, Ferdinando's eldest daughter, received extensive holdings in the distribution, including several manors and large estates in England and Wales.

In January 1595, Earl William was married in London to Elizabeth, the eldest daughter of Edward Vere, the seventeenth earl of Oxford, by whom he had three sons and three daughters. Queen Elizabeth conferred upon him the Noble Order of the Garter. From 1594 to 1618, this Derby maintained a troupe of actors known as Derby's Men, not to be confused with the earlier groups, his brother's Strange's Men, and the earlier Fourth Earl's Derby's Men. Earl William's Men made appearances at court and toured the provinces. There is a report that he wrote plays, which is possible, but the idea that he was the author of the plays ascribed to Shakespeare is untenable.

Here we come to the circumstances of the writing, purpose and first performance of Shakespeare's ever-popular play *A Midsummer Night's Dream*. Harold F. Brooks, in his Arden Shakespeare edition of the play (Routledge, 1993) writes, 'Most scholars are agreed that the *Dream* was designed to grace a wedding in a noble household' (introduction, p. liii). An (admittedly old-fashioned) edition of the play published by Cambridge University Press in 1924, edited by Sir Arthur Quiller-Couch and John Dover Wilson (introduction, p. XV) tries the following:

> In all modesty, to get at the workings of Shakespeare's mind ... Here (say we) we have a young playwright commissioned to write a wedding-play—a play to be presented in some great private house before a distinguished company. He has patrons to conciliate, favour to win, his own ambitions to set in a fair road of success. He is naturally anxious to shine; here is his opportunity; and, moreover, though his fellow playwrights already pay him the compliment of being a little jealous, he still has his spurs to win. 'Upstart crow am I? You wait a bit, my supercilious University wits, and see what a countryman can make, up from Warwickshire ... one must not introduce topical hits or malice in

celebrating a bridal ... a wedding, if any occasion on earth, should be human: what is more, a wedding above any occasion on earth calls for poetry—and I can write poetry—witness my *Venus and Adonis* ... the sweethearting must be fresh ... A night for lovers ... the moon ... Pitch darkness is for tragedy, moonlight for love, for illusion ... real Warwickshire fairies ... How does that verse by Spenser go?—'Ne let the Pouke'.

... One of the editors once discussed with a friend how, if given their will, they would have *A Midsummer Night's Dream* presented. They agreed at length on this: The set scene should represent a large Elizabethan hall, panelled, having a lofty oak-timbered roof and an enormous staircase. The cavity under the staircase, occupying in breadth two-thirds of the stage, should be fronted with folding or sliding doors, which being opened, should reveal the wood, recessed, moonlit, with its trees upon a flat arras or tapestry. On this secondary remoter stage the lovers should wander through their adventures, the fairies now conspiring in the quiet hall ... For the last scene the hall should be filled with lights and company. That over, the bridal couples go up the great staircase. Last of all ... [the hall] lit by a flicker from the hearth— the fairies, announced by Puck, should come tripping back, swarming forth from cupboards and down curtains, somersaulting downstairs, sliding down the bannister rails.

... Oberon instructs, 'Through the house give glimmering light.' Titania replies, 'Hand in hand with fairy grace/We will sing and bless this place.' Oberon leads the fairies in the final song and dance: 'And each several chamber bless/Through this Palace with sweet peace./And the owner of it bless'd/Ever shall in safety rest.'

This final section (after Puck has offered 'To sweep the dust behind the door') has a strong sense of a real room in a real house or palace; indeed, a 'large Elizabethan hall', as Quiller-Couch and Dover Wilson proposed. The 'owner' of the palace in the play is Theseus, but his name does not appear in this final section. It is as though the original hall where the play was first presented has taken over. The word 'owner' is curiously pointed, as is 'palace' where we might expect 'house'. The repetition of the word 'bless' (lines 47–49) is rather obtrusive unless it has a secondary function. Hearing this, following the rhyme, does not the mind slip over to the word 'Bess'? Was this not what ordinary people affectionately called their Queen: Good Queen Bess? 'Palace' is redolent of the Queen's palace at Greenwich; it was always called 'Greenwich Palace', where some scholars say Shakespeare's *A Midsummer Night's Dream* was first performed. It is likely, therefore, that Shakespeare's text was written to be performed before Queen Bess (Elizabeth) at her palace at Greenwich.

The great scholar E. K. Chambers, in his essay 'The Occasion of *A Midsummer Night's Dream*' (*Shakespearean Gleanings*, Oxford, 1944) writes:

It has long been recognized that the epithalmic ending of *A Midsummer Night's Dream* points to performance at a wedding, and that the compliment to the 'fair vestal throned by the west' points to a wedding at which Queen Elizabeth was present. The most plausible date hitherto suggested is 26 January 1595, on which William Stanley, Earl of Derby, married the Lady Elizabeth Vere, daughter of the Earl of Oxford, granddaughter of William, Lord Burley, and goddaughter and maid of honour to the queen. This would fit in well enough with the allusions in the play to the bad weather of 1594 and to the lion at the baptism of Prince Henry of Scotland on 30 August of the same year; while the presence of Elizabeth has been inferred from the words of Stowe, who says that 'The 26 of January William Earl of Derby married the Earl of Oxford's daughter at the court then at Greenwich, which marriage feast was there most royally kept.' (p. 61)

However, Chambers thinks Stowe was mistaken with respect to the location of the wedding, that in fact 'it took place at Burley House in the Strand and that the marriage was solemnised at the Chapel of the Savoy nearby':

The much-travelled Theseus might have been thought appropriate to William Stanley, whose own travels are said to have taken him as far as the Holy Land and Russia, and in later Lancashire legends grew to quite mythical proportions ... the water-pageant [Act II Scene 1 pp. 147–170] ... is far more likely to have been that which had occurred comparatively recently, when Elizabeth visited the Earl of Hertford at Elvetham in September 1591 ... it is to cupid and the wound inflicted by his bolt on the little western flower that the whole description leads up.... if it points to an enamoured woman ... how can it be anybody else but be the bride in whose glorification, next only to that of Elizabeth, the play was written? ... Elizabeth Vere, as one of the queen's maids, is at least likely to have been there, and William Stanley, who was coming and going in 1589 and 1590 between London and his father's houses in the north, may quite well have been there too ... Burghley, perhaps the greatest of our civil servants, had the civil servant's not uncommon foible for founding a dynasty. It was in 1594 that the deaths in rapid succession of his father and his elder brother left Stanley the most eligible match in England.

An explanation for the title of the play is as follows: that in English folklore midsummer was traditionally the best time for a wedding. Ancient belief marked the earlier months of the year as male (ploughing, sowing, etc.) and the later months as female (conceiving, growing, giving birth, nurturing, etc.). Midsummer Day, about 24 June, was the day mythically and really conjoining the two equally and fortuitously.

Most of the action of the play takes place on Mayday. As on Midsummer Night, this was a period when supernatural events abounded, when fairies were thought to be particularly powerful and when magic and witchcraft were practised. Midsummer, however, had special qualities: herbs and flowers gathered on that night possessed magic powers. Shakespeare conflates them, creating a fictional world from the two most potent festive periods of the traditional rural year.

Charles Squire writes:

> Whatever may be the exact meaning of the Celtic state worship, there seems to be no doubt that it centred around the four great days in the year which chronicle the rise, progress and decline of the sun, and therefore the fruits of the earth. These were: Beltaine, which fell at the beginning of May; Midsummer Day, marking the triumph of sunshine and vegetation ... If anything uncanny took place, it was sure to be on May-day ... Beltaine, Calan Mai in Wales ... celebrates the waking of the earth from her winter sleep and the renewal of warmth, life and vegetation ... the festival was so eagerly anticipated that no-one could sleep upon its eve. At midnight the people rose, and, going to the nearest woods, tore down the branches of trees, with which the sun, when he rose, would find doors and windows decked for him. They spent the day in dancing around the May-pole, with rude, rustic mirth, man joining with nature to celebrate the coming of summer. (pp. 407–8)

In his Arden edition of *A Midsummer Night's Dream*, Harold Brooks writes:

> It seems likely that Queen Elizabeth was present when the *Dream* was first acted ... [the marriage] was solemnised at Greenwich where the court then was; the Queen is known to have honoured with her presence the wedding festivities at Burghley House in the Strand. Elizabeth Vere was Lord Burghley's granddaughter and one of the Queen's maids of honour. (introduction, p. lvi).

It is, according to contemporary records, the only wedding the Queen ever attended. The text of the play supports the presence of the Queen; it was written in 1594. It may well be that Stowe's account is correct and that Her Majesty did not need to go out to the wedding, that she stayed at home to enjoy dancing and the first performance of Shakespeare's specially written play.

In contemporary Elizabethan thought, the moon was associated with their Queen, and there are over twenty separate allusions to the moon in this play, such as in Act 1, Scene 1:

> ... Thrice blessed they that master so their blood
> To undergo such maiden pilgrimage;

But earthlier happy is the rose distilled
Than that which, withering on the virgin thorn
Grows, lives and dies in single blessedness.

The pointed compliment 'Thrice blessed' echoes '[Queen] Bess': Queen Elizabeth. It is she who possesses the 'rose distilled'; hers is not the less happy 'single blessedness' but a multiple, rare, one, 'distilled' in to something superior. The key to this passage is 'master': one who controls her natural passions for a good end is a superior person. This is not a criticism of Elizabeth, as some have believed, but a compliment.

It seems very likely that the Queen attended some part of the marriage events. The bride was part of her retinue, and a direct descendant of one of her principal courtiers. William was from of a powerful and wealthy noble family. From the way in which the play is couched, Shakespeare had a performance at a 'palace' with grounds in mind: Elizabeth's Greenwich Palace is a likely venue. Burleigh's comment about dancing is indicative of an event in which the Queen's love of dancing would find expression.

Identification with the Stanley family could be established in Theseus's first speech:

This old moon wanes: she lingers my desires
Like to a stepdame or a dowager
Long withering out a young man's revenue.

The contemporary audience would have understood this as an allusion to dowager Alice Stanley holding on to her late husband's possessions as long as possible rather than allowing them to pass on to William. It is very unlikely that Alice attended this wedding, given the animosity between her and William. 'Widow aunt, dowager' appears again in line 157 of Act 1 scene 1. The contemporary audience would have enjoyed the double joke. Theseus, at the beginning says, 'Hyppolyta, I wooed thee with my sword,/And won thy love doing thee injuries'. They would be reminded of William's fantastical travels and his alleged prowess with a sword. That Hyppolyta is said to have been 'captured' abroad during Theseus's travels and that she was one of the bold warlike tribe of 'Amazons' further gently mocks William's pretentions and humorously comments on Elizabeth, she being in every probability a very English, urbane, courtly figure, of a gentle nature and certainly not Amazonian.

Titania's speech about bad weather (Act II, scene 1) seems to be a description of the bad weather of 1594, described in Robert Parry's diary. This helps to identify the period of composition.

An additional detail on the matter of the Elvetham (Hampshire) entertainment of September 1591 (when Queen Elizabeth made one of her rare and expensive visits to provincial noble houses) is on a contemporary illustration, which shows the Queen sitting as on a throne on the western rim of the specially dug moon-shaped lake with the word 'WEST' clearly inscribed on the edge of the map close to a raised and canopied platform: her 'throne'. Additionally, at least thirty courtly ladies and gentlemen are depicted about the lake's margin, some of them standing close together holding hands. It seems certain that some ladies-in-waiting were 'courting'. One of these was in all probability Elizabeth de Vere, and her young man could have been William Stanley (although we have no proof of their presence). The 'fair vestal' of the text would be Queen Elizabeth, the famous 'maiden' ('And the imperial votress passed on/In maiden meditation, fancy free'). She is missed by cupid's arrow, being the 'virgin queen', but the 'little western flower' (as distinct from the large one who would be the Queen; the parallelism reinforced by their same name) who is hit is, according to our thesis, Elizabeth de Vere. It is a reasonable hypothesis that Shakespeare knew of this event and saw this drawing of it. A printed account of the entertainment complete with the illustration of the lake's events was published by John Wolfe ('and are to bee sold at the Little Shop over against the great South Dore of Paules') in late 1591.

The Earls of Derby enjoyed country sports. The hounds that feature in this play are easily associated with those bred by retainers of the Stanleys. A central symbolism plays on the sound of the baying of the hounds, firstly discordant, then concordant, as the action of the play moves from discord to harmony. 'My love,' says Theseus, 'shall hear the music of my hounds./Uncouple in the Western valley, let them go' (IV, 1, 109–10). This second line would be addressed away from Hippolyta, in a different tone, as if he was giving direct orders to his retainers, from the Master Forester of Wirral, which William, the Sixth Earl, actually was. (Oberon: 'I with the Morning's Love have oft made sport/ And like a Forester the Groves may tread' *MND*, III, 2, 388–9) 'Western' would make sense because the Wirral and its forests are to the west of Lancashire.

An interesting reference to the prevalence and superiority of Lancashire hounds is made by Gervase Markham in his 'Countrey Contentments' of 1612. He writes:

If you would have your kennel for depth of mouth, then you shall compound it of the largest dogs, which have the greatest mouths and deepest flews, such as your west-country Cheshire and Lancashire dogs are.

He then proceeds to describe 'the music of … hounds':

And to five or six couple of bass mouths you shall not add above two couple of counter-tenors, as many means, and not above one couple of roarers, which being heard but now and then, as at the opening or hitting of a scent, will give much sweetness to the solemness and graveness of the cry, and the music thereof will be much more delightful to the ears of every beholder.

Harold F. Brooks (introduction, p. lxxiii) writes the following in his discussion of the play's fairies:

Giraldus Cambrensis relates how Elidorus was taken to a fairy kingdom with inhabitants of the smallest stature, their horses being the size of hares ... The Tylwyth Teg ('the fair Tribe') are among the principal fairies of Wales, and are commonly reputed to dance on the tops of rushes, or in a ring, sometimes by the light of a glow-worm, or to hide in the fox-glove ... there is ample reason to think that Shakespeare would know of the Welsh fairies themselves: it is plain that in 1595–9 he was interested in matters Welsh.

Brooks's translation of Tylwyth Teg is in fact slightly wrong; a more accurate translation would be 'the fair family' ('teulu' is Welsh for family). A good account of these Welsh fairies appears in *Welsh Legends and fairy Lore* (D. Parry-Jones, Batsford, 1953) where the author places the Cambrensis account of Elidorus finding a subterranean passage to fairy-land in the Vale of Neath. Typical traditional Welsh fairies are virtuous, truthful and live in families; they are unselfish, caring for one another: this may be behind Oberon's comment in Act III 'But we are spirits of another sort'—spirits, that is, of light, virtue and co-operation, not 'Damned spirits' that appear as ghosts in churchyards and appear where criminals are buried at cross-roads. However, the unpleasant tradition of the changeling child, which Shakespeare knew, persists even among these Welsh fairies: when a human child (always male) is stolen and taken to fairyland and a fairy child is left in its place.

We know that the north Wales historian (buried in Ruabon church) and Church of England clergyman David Powel (1552?–1598) published his *Historie of Cambria* in 1584. This text cites William Cecil, Lord Burghley, as one who aided Powel, giving him access to official records. In 1585, Powel published three books in a single volume: this included *Itinerarium Cambriae* and the *Descriptio Cambriae* of Giraldus Cambrensis. This was the first printed text of Giraldus. The text of *Itinerarium* (in Latin) includes the account of Elidorus's access through a cave to the world of the fairies.

A copy of this book may have been bought for the Stanley library. Also, it may have been in the library at Lleweni. If Shakespeare was there at Christmas 1593–1594, he may have read it. He would have had sufficient Latin to do so. It is very possible that this text influenced his distinctive shaping of the fairy world of *A Midsummer Night's Dream*.

The Vale of Neath has been associated with fairies. Geraldus says that Elidorus, a priest, when he was twelve, ran away and hid under a riverbank.

Two men of small stature stood before him and invited him to go with them. He followed a path, partly underground, and came to a beautiful valley; the days were cloudy and the nights very dark. The boy was brought before the King and his court and he was given a young boy.

> These fairy people were of fair complexion and had luxuriant hair falling over their shoulders like that of women. They had horses and greyhounds adapted to their size. They ate no flesh but lived on a milk diet. They detested lies and disapproved of the human world's ambition, infidelities and inconsistencies. The boy at one time went back to his mother's home in the real world, having stolen a ball of gold, which the fairies recovered. He never found his way back to the fairy world. (See an English translation by R. C. Hoare published by Everyman in 1908; reissued 1976).

Many factors, therefore, point to the strong possibility that Shakespeare's *A Midsummer Night's Dream* was a play, if not commissioned for, then written for, the marriage of William, the Sixth Earl of Derby, and Elizabeth de Vere, which took place in London on 26 January 1595.

The Chambers Accounts of 5 March 1595 show that Shakespeare, Kempe, and R. Burbage were paid for two performances at Greenwich Palace on 26–27 December 1594. We do not know which play or plays were put on. At this point in time, William would have left the Stanley entourage and become a Chamberlain's Man. However, he (if our thesis is correct) would have owed a great deal to the Stanleys and when the marriage of one of them was proposed, he would have no hesitation in offering his services as a playwright, composing a piece to be performed on the evening of the wedding day.

14

Plutarch's *Lives* Gifted to a Man Called William

It is well known that he depended upon the plots, and even the words, of others; he lifted passages from North and borrowed images from Ovid. There is hardly a play of his which is not established upon some earlier source, historical or dramatic, so that he corresponds to the English archetype; he seems most original when he borrows most freely. Like the language and the nation itself he is altogether receptive, taking up external or foreign constituents and moulding them instinctively to his purpose.

Peter Ackroyd, *Albion*, p. 222

In the quiet, wood-panelled environs of the Shakespeare Birthplace Trust, Henley Street, Stratford-upon-Avon, Warwickshire, protected in a time-locked vault, is the volume that is the subject of this chapter.

It is Plutarch's *Lives*. When it was acquired by this library in 1985 from Pickering and Chatto (ref 658 at SR.0S 97), it was entered in their catalogue as follows:

NORTH, Sir Thomas, translator. THE LIVES OF THE NOBLE GRECIANS AND ROMANES, compared together by that graue learned philosopher and historiographer, Plutarke of Chaeronea: translated out of Greeke into French by Iames Amyot, Abbot of Bellozane, Bishop of Auxerre, one of the Kings priuy counsel, and great Amner of France, and out of French into Englishe, by Thomas North. Imprinted at London by Thomas Vautroullier and Iohn Wight. 1579.

The book dealers wrote:

FIRST EDITION. Folio, [xii], pp. 1,172 ... several inscriptions of the title and one or two marks in the text (see below), a few stains in the main text but generally a surprisingly clean copy, rebound at an early stage by a provincial or even amateur binder in panelled calf.

Plutarch (*c.* 50–120) was a Roman historian and writer. He was a teacher and he gained the patronage of the Emperor Trajan. He wrote his *Parallel Lives*, his most celebrated work, forty-six scholarly biographies of famous Greeks and Romans, nearly all arranged in pairs: e.g. Theseus and Romulous as founders of states. It was translated by Sir Thomas North (?1535–?1601) from the French version of Jacques Amyot.

North's *Plutarch* was one of the most influential books of its age. It gave Shakespeare much source-material, particularly for *Julius Caesar, Timon of Athens, Coriolanus,* and *Antony and Cleopatra*. Halliday writes:

> Sometimes he takes long passages of North's prose and puts them into blank verse with little change, though he nearly always adds some touch that transfigures the whole. The death of Charmian [Cleopatra's servant] is a good illustration of Shakespeare's following of North, and of the addition of two words of Shakespearean magic:

> [North]
> One of the soldiers, seeing her, angrily said unto her; 'Is that well done, Charmion?' 'Very well,' said she again, 'and meet for a princess descended from the race of so many noble kings.' She said no more, but fell down dead by the bed.

> [Shakespeare]
> GUARD. What work is here! Charmian, is this well done?

> CHAR. It is well done, and fitting for a princess
>   Descended of so many royal kings.
>   Ah, soldier! [Dies.]

> *A Shakespeare Companion*, p. 338

The most famous parallel passage is in *Antony and Cleopatra* (II.ii):

> [North]
> She disdained to set forward otherwise, but to take her barge in the river of Cydnus, the poope whereof was of gold, the sails of purple, and the owers of silver, which kept stroke in rowing after the sound of flutes, howboys, cythern, violls, and such other instruments as they played upon the barge.

[Shakespeare]
The barge she sat in like a burnish'd throne,
Burn'd on the water: the poop was beaten gold;
Purple the sails, and so perfumed that
The winds were love-sick with them; the oars were silver,
Which to the tune of flutes kept stroke, and made
The water which they beat to follow faster,
As amorous of their strokes ...

Earlier plays, such as *Titus Andronicus* and *A Midsummer Night's Dream*, also show the influence of North's work: information about Theseus's various loves in *A Midsummer Night's Dream* is drawn from North.

The present copy of North belonged to the Earls of Derby. It was given to the fourth Earl, Henry Stanley (1531–1593) by William Chaderton (1540?–1608), Bishop of Chester, and it was given away by Alice Spencer (d. 1637), wife of Ferdinando (1560–1594), Fifth Earl.

Henry, the Fourth Earl, died in September 1593 and his eldest son and heir Ferdinando died in April 1594. Ferdinando's players were subsequently taken over by his dowager, Alice, until the Chamberlain's Men playing group was formed in June 1594. These details and the circumstances surrounding the likely composition by Shakespeare of *A Midsummer Night's Dream* during 1594, in anticipation of the William–Elizabeth marriage [q.v.], leads us to speculate that this important book was given by Alice to new playwright William Shakespeare in the months following September 1593 and that he used it when writing *Dream* (intermittently) in late 1593 and through 1594.

The gift of this volume to a 'William' is made very clear by an annotation on the title page. After the first six lines of annotation, stating the Chaderton/ Derby ownership (mentioned above), comes a second three-line annotation; but this one, very interestingly, is heavily overscored with circular pen strokes, but can be read with the aid of a magnifying glass. It reads:

Nunc Wilhelmi
Dono Nobilissima
Alisiae Comitissae

This can be translated as follows:

Now William
By the most generous gift
Countess Alice

To whom, then, was the present volume given? William, the Fifth Earl, might be thought to be this 'William', but relations between him and Alice were so strained that this is very unlikely. She had called him a 'nidicock'.

The rapid development of playing companies, involving those of the Stanleys, through this seminal period, and the consequent pressure to create new plays, leads one to give credence to the proposition that William Shakespeare was the recipient of this volume.

A third inscription appears on the volume, thus: 'Edw: Stanly. 1611'. This Edward Stanley (1562–1623) was the son of Sir Thomas Stanley (d. 1576), the latter being the second son of the Third Earl of Derby. Shakespeare is believed to be the author of inscriptions on this family's tomb of St Edward at Tong Church, Staffordshire.

So, the book was back in the possession of the Derbys in 1611. If the book had been in Shakespeare's library from 1593 to 1611, that would be consistent with what we have said about his work and his life. In returning the book, a courtesy typical of the man, in 1611 or earlier (when he no longer needed it), we recognise a gesture consistent with the ending of his active writing life and (brought on largely, as we have suggested, by his 'writer's palsy') the beginning of his 'retirement'.

Except (and here we make a short diversion) I do not believe he 'retired to Stratford' as some biographies so blandly assert. I believe he spent most of his last years in London, where he had bought a house in 1613 and where his friend John Robinson lived, according to Shakespeare's will. Robinson was a signatory of the will of January and March 1616, drawn up, almost certainly in Stratford, using the services of a lawyer. The likely chronology is as follows: in January, at his house in Stratford-upon-Avon, Shakespeare dictates to a clerk the first draft his will. Shakespeare returns to London; he falls ill; he returns to Stratford in March accompanied by John Robinson; the rough copy is brought to him; he dictates amendments; his illness worsens; there is fear for his life and rather than waiting for the lawyer's clerk to return to his office to create an immaculate final draft and bring it to Stratford for signature; the old draft three leaves are produced; and Shakespeare signs all three pages, page three first but his signature is marred by his writer's palsy, thus the poor signatures on pages one and two. The inscription 'By me William Shakespeare' authenticates the will's author. Local witnesses are brought in and, to make certain that the future of the London house, the Blackfriars Gatehouse, is secure according to the will's instructions, John Robinson is asked to sign as a witness.

I therefore believe that even though Shakespeare was forced to retire from writing plays (although he could still dictate, as I believe he did to John Fletcher, the presumed co-author of Shakespeare's last play, albeit a collaboration, *Henry VIII* of 1612), he did not retire from the life of the theatre, which was centred on London. This play was performed on 29 June 1613 at the Globe, when (rather fittingly, bringing down the curtain on Shakespeare's career as a playwright) it burned down.

Now we return to the North volume. Did Shakespeare handwrite the second inscription in North? He could have done. The lines are in italic script. The line '*dono Nobilissima*' ('by the most generous gift') is couched in the language of patronage and suggests, in its fulsomeness, a giftee of lower social and economic standing. It seems likely that this William had composed this wording himself, if not handwritten it himself. There is a fair chance, therefore, that this inscription—given that he was the book's recipient—was handwritten in the book by Shakespeare, using, very unusually, italic script (which in the Elizabethan period was used by the higher-born and higher-educated for the most prestigious parts of their handwritten texts, particularly signatures). Shakespeare's extant signatures are not formed in italic, but he was an experienced scribe and the chances are that he could execute italic. The handwriting in the North volume—given the exalted position of its owners—might be a special case of displaying gratitude in handwriting in a form which the well-educated nobility used and which matched the style of the first six-line inscription.

15

The Passionate Pilgrim

E. K. Chambers describes this volume as follows: '[Octavo 1.1599.] The Passionate Pilgrime. By W. Shakespeare. [Ornament] At London Printed >by Thomas Judson< for W. Iaggard, and are to be sold by W. Leake, at the Greyhound in Paules Churchyard. 1599.' (p. 547) A later edition is thus described: '[O3.1612.] The Passionate Pilgrime Or Certaine Amorous Sonnets, betweene Venus and Adonis, newly corrected and augmented. By W. Shakespeare'.

All this illustrates 'the battle of the books'. By this time, in 1599, Shakespeare's name was well-known; publishers and printers, especially the none too scrupulous ones, were keen to cash in on it. The original publisher of the sonnets (Thorpe) rushed it to print as soon as he got his hands on the manuscript; Shakespeare almost certainly did not supervise the final printed text. Had he done so, he would almost certainly have excised Thorp's eccentric and unscrupulous dedication.

There are twenty short poems in *The Passionate Pilgrim* and very little is Shakespeare's. There is little doubt that the rather clumsy hand of Bartholomew Griffin (d. 1602) appears here; also present is the rather more accomplished hand of Richard Barnfield, and it may well be the case that they were friends of Shakespeare's and John Salusbury's. Salusbury's quite accomplished poem (marked IV, p. 7 of the Carleton Brown volume) 'Of late I went my dearest ...' seems to be echoed in some of the Griffin-ascribed poems in *The Passionate Pilgrim*. It would not be surprising if Griffin wrote much of his material after hearing of the John Salusbury–Dorothy Halsall infatuation and reading some of John's poems that incorporate it. The circumstances of 'A Lover's Complaint' seem similar to the settings and narrative of the Venus and Adonis' clerk poems here (IV; VI; VII; IX; and XI).

Peter Levi, in his *The Life and Times of William Shakespeare* (Macmillan, 1988), writes perceptively, 'The Adonis sonnets printed later in *The Passionate Pilgrim* (1599) look like the relics of a game among friends dating from the time when he wrote *Venus and Adonis*.' These friends could have come together in London (John Salusbury was a frequent visitor).

However, our particular interest now is the poem XV, which is here quoted in full:

> *It was a lording's daughter, the fairest one of three,*
> *That liked of her master as well as well might be,*
> *Till looking on an Englishman, the fairest that eye could see,*
> *Her fancy fell a-turning.*
> *Long was the combat doubtful, that love with love did fight,*
> *To leave the master loveless, or kill the gallant knight;*
> *To put in practice either, alas, it was a spite*
> *Unto the silly damsel!*
> *But one must be refused; more mickle was the pain,*
> *That nothing could be used to turn them both to gain,*
> *For of the two the trusty knight was wounded with disdain:*
> *Alas, she could not help it!*
> *Thus art with arms contending was victor of the day,*
> *Which by a gift of learning did bear the maid away:*
> *Then lullaby, the learned man hath got the lady gay;*
> *For now my song is ended.*

This is clearly not a good poem—it is clumsy, unclear, and incoherent; it also has very limited diction and a bathetic ending. It is very unlikely to have come from the pen of Shakespeare. Our interest here, however, is in its content, narrative, and setting. The first line is especially interesting: 'It was a lording's daughter, the fairest one of three'. Who was the 'lording' with three daughters? A clear candidate for this particular reference would be Ferdinando, Lord Strange. Before his father died in 1593, he could be described as a 'lording'—a minor lord, so to speak, to his father's major Lord. His three daughters were Anne (b. 1580), who (firstly) married Grey (Brydges) Baron Chandos; Frances, who married John Egerton and became Countess of Bridgewater; and Elizabeth, who married Henry Hastings, becoming Countess of Huntingdon. An entry in the *Complete Peerage* makes this interesting point:

> The representation of Lady Chandos is very obscure, which is remarkable, inasmuch as if Edward Seymour ... be considered illegitimate ... the Crown would have vested in her [Anne's] issue after the death of Queen Elizabeth under the will of Henry VIII (made in accordance with Act of Parl.), which excluded the Scottish line ... (p. 213)

Then, back to our poem: who was 'the fairest one of three'? Could it be Anne, the most eligible and the eldest? The next line may afford us a clue: 'That liked of her master as well as well might be'. 'Master' can be read as 'schoolmaster', a usage extant at the time. We are reminded of Beeston's comment about 'a schoolmaster in the country'. Could this line refer to William Shakespeare, schoolmaster in the Stanley household, and that he was Anne's schoolmaster? 'A gift of learning' would be a suitable epithet for William Shakespeare. We have already speculated that in 1582–1586, he was especially hard-pressed for an income and might well have taken up paid employment as a teacher. This possible association with Anne Stanley is echoed at the end of the 'Denbigh Poem' (see chapters 16 and 17) where, after an encomium to John and Ursula Stanley, the author enthusiastically (and very out of context) greets a certain Anne Stanley.

The comment 'Till looking on an Englishman' suggests somebody 'very English', which is consistent with Lord Chandos. 'Art with arms' indicates an artistic man competing for her love with a 'knight', meaning a man of high social standing, 'arms' meaning coat of arms. The man with a 'gift of learning' however is victor and the 'trusty knight' is defeated: 'wounded with disdain'. Was William Shakespeare the 'learned' man? It is possible. We have to assume that tables were turned, that the maid dropped her 'master'. and later took up with either this Englishman, or another. Such a high-born girl would not in all probability marry her schoolmaster, actor, and playwright.

When did the Anne-Grey Brydges relationship occur? We do not know for certain but Levi reports that the poet and satirist John Marston composed what appears to be a masque under the heading *The Entertainment of the Dowager Countess of Derby* which was performed in late July or early August 1607 for the engagement of her eldest daughter Anne, to Lord Chandos.

We may remind ourselves at this point that the most famous, and considered by many experts in the field to be the most authentic, painting of William Shakespeare, is called 'The Chandos Portrait'. The painting was in other hands earlier, but the acquisition of this portrait by James Brydges, the Third Duke of Chandos, in 1789, may be linked with the marriage of Anne Stanley and Baron Chandos in 1607. The family may have acquired it as a token of appreciation for the young man with a 'gift for learning' who was a private tutor to the young 'Ane stanley'.

16

'The Denbigh Poem': Part One

According to Tom Lloyd-Roberts ('Bard of Lleweni? Shakespeare's Welsh Connection' *The New Welsh Review* No. 23 Winter 1993–1994), 'it seems likely that the young John Salusbury and William Shakespeare first became acquainted in either late 1586 or early 1587'.

We recall that in the autumn of 1586 John Salusbury's elder brother, Thomas, was put to death and in December John married Ursula. We have speculated that the young Shakespeare, resident under the Stanleys at Lathom, had a close knowledge of both events.

In 1588, Lord Leicester died and the patronage of his company of players was taken over by Ursula Salusbury's half-brother Ferdinando, Lord Strange. John and Ursula eventually named one of their sons Ferdinando. John's interests at Oxford were poetry and boxing or wrestling; he was known as 'John the Strong'. Then, at the age of twenty, when his grandfather died, he inherited the estates of the Salusburys. The signs are he divided his time largely between Lleweni and London, while Ursula stayed at Lleweni, bearing his children in every year from 1587 to 1600, except for four years (1591, 1593, 1596, and 1598). In 1594, at the age of twenty-eight, John was admitted as a student to the Middle Temple and in April 1597, he was appointed by the Privy Council Deputy Lieutenant for the County of Denbigh. A recommendation from the Earl of Pembroke, Lord President of Wales, stated that John Salusbury was 'a gentleman of good livlyhood and by longe continuance of his auncestours well esteemed in the Country and also Her Majesty's servant'. Then, four years later, in June 1601, he was knighted personally by the Queen, a signal honour so late in her reign. The reinstatement of the Salusburys in public was complete.

We now come to Christ Church MSS 183 and 184, which by permission of an erstwhile assistant librarian of Christ Church, Oxford, are reproduced here both in their original manuscript form and in printed form, the latter taken from the Brown volume. These manuscripts were once at Lleweni and were pasted in to the commonplace volume of the Salusbury household (the

A page from the Salusbury papers at Bangor University Archives showing songs and tunes played at a Christmas celebration, dated bottom right 1593, sometimes read as 1595.

Salusbury Volume), which contained a collection of verses in Welsh, English, and Latin, mainly in praise of John Salusbury and his family. This volume was bound in leather in the early seventeenth century: it is in the library of Christ Church, Oxford. What concerns us here are the 'Danielle' poems, which are MS 184, folios eighty-two and eighty-three. For simplicity of nomenclature, I have called the writing on these three pages (two leaves) 'The Denbigh Poem', which is in two parts. It is written in a small, heavy hand, very neatly and clearly, by the same person; this hand does not appear elsewhere in the collection. The same hand, in italic script, has written *'finis quoth* Danielle' under both sections, and, in the case of the second part, below an obliterated piece of writing. The striking through is heavy and made with horizontal strokes seemingly with the same ink as that underneath, making it exceedingly difficult to try to decipher what was put down originally. It looks as if the author wrote something at the end of the poem, then changed his mind, obliterated it, and inserted the Danielle phrase twice, instead.

The paper size is 29 cm by 19 cm; there is no visible watermark. The paper itself is of the 'laid' type (displaying fine horizontal lines within it), substantial and of high quality. The first part of the poem is on the front (recto) of leaf eighty-two, consisting of fifty-four lines and on the reverse of this leaf (verso) with eighteen lines, followed by *'finis quoth* Danielle' in italic. The second part of the poem is on leaf eighty-three, recto only, consisting of thirty lines, followed by the obliterated writing and overscoring. Each stanza of six lines through the poem is separated by a hand-drawn horizontal line.

Whose handwriting is this? It is, as has been said, like no other writing in this huge volume of collected writings. A poem by Ben Jonson is here, in his own handwriting. This paper is folded in the same way as 'The Denbigh Poem'. This suggests that both sets of papers originated in one place, say in London, were then folded and placed in a pocket or satchel, and then taken, probably by horse, to a place some distance away, (the folds are prominent, suggesting pressure over a period of time), consistent with Denbigh.

The first section of the poem was written by someone (call him 'G' for guest) who had visited Lleweni, Denbigh. He writes twelve stanzas of six lines each in the regular rhyme-scheme ABABCC (the same form as Shakespeare's *Venus and Adonis*). In these seventy-two lines, there is no mention of Ursula by name although she appears allegorically as Helen. The name Salusbury appears twenty times, each time written in italic. This was a convention of the period; it appears in playscripts and legal documents. It is a feature of the script of the manuscript copy of *Edmund Ironside*.

We have to distinguish between the handwriting and the poem itself as a literary construct: the author of the poem is not necessarily the person who handwrote it. The author—'G'—is writing an encomium (a poem of high-flown praise). He praises John Salusbury repeatedly: 'free of his purse, the flowre of all his kine'; 'the onely perle which all prowd wale doth foyle'; 'is not Salusbury the manliest wight in Britaine you can find'; and so on. 'G' has definitely visited the Salusbury home in Denbigh: 'Denbighe adew pray thou for Salusbury/north wales adew pray ye for Salusbury'. He knew John's reputation for strength: 'His manlike armes ffrom of the greekish wales/would tosse down pilleres like to tennis bales.'

'G' is an eccentric speller. Then, we run into a problem. Was the putative scribe an eccentric speller? Was he copying 'G's script exactly, including the odd spellings? Shakespeare had a number of peculiar spelling habits, according to J. Dover Wilson and New York handwriting expert Charles Hamilton. According to Hamilton, one of them consisted of putting down a 'e' when there was no call for it. This version of 'The Denbigh Poem' is full of redundant 'e's: 'quakinge'; 'standes'; 'egge'; 'Goe'; 'tosse'; 'treadinge'; 'lowe'; 'blesse'; and 'heare'. Another peculiarity is using 'y' and 'i' interchangeably—in this script we have: 'vayne'; 'soyle'; 'foyle'; 'lyes'; 'liueinge'; 'wynne'; 'nimphes'; and 'myddest'. Another is the habit of interchanging 'u' and 'v'—this script has: 'mvses'; 'leaue'; 'vnlike'; 'siluer'; 'euer'; and 'mvst', etc. There is the doubling of a final consonant: 'forgott'; 'putt', etc., which is a Shakespearean habit, as is the uncertainty about a single and double 'f': 'ffeare'; 'ffayne'; 'ffrom'; and 'ffor', etc. Also note the single medial consonant in 'ofspringe'; the interchangeable 'c', 's', and 'z' as in 'The Denbigh Poem's 'practize'; and the interchangeable 'e', 'ei', and 'ie': 'prayeinge' and 'liueinge'. All these peculiarities of 'The Denbigh Poem' are typical of Shakespeare's way of writing. It seems, given these eccentricities, that the script is not the work of a scrivener; he would presumably have 'corrected' these scripting 'errors'.

There are many abbreviations in this handwritten text, which is unusual in such a formal presentation, including 'tis' and 'twere' (which are frequent in Shakespeare's Quartos, according to Dover Wilson); and a distinctive ampersand with a short tittle running down to the line with a heavy curved stroke below it resembling a 'c'. There is here a distinctive abbreviation for 'your' and for 'mistress'.

Take, for instance, A Midsummer Night's Dream, Act 2, scene 1, line 183: 'And ere I take this charm from off her sight'. The editors of the Cambridge edition, Quiller-Couch and Dover Wilson, note that this 'off' is a 'Shakespearian spelling'. (p. 116). The same peculiar 'from off' appears in our Denbigh Poem: 'from off the Greekish wales'.

Stanza twelve includes: 'dianas trayne'; 'silver'; 'nymph'; and 'dance'. These are in the spirit of A Midsummer Night's Dream, as follows: 'Dian's bud oe'r Cupid's flower' (4.1); 'And then the moon, like to a silver bow' (1.1); and 'When Phoebe doth behold/Her silver Visage in the wat'ry glass' (1.1). The line in 'G's stanza twelve, 'The nimphes shall dance', echoes the play's 'Fare thee well nymph' (2.1). The nymphs are dancing in 'The Denbigh Poem' and in A

Midsummer Night's Dream: 'If you will patiently daunce in our Round' (2.1); 'Come now, a Roundel' (2.2); and 'I'll lead you about a Round'. In 'The Denbigh Poem', we have 'coridon's roondelays'. This is from the French 'rondele'.

Parallel texts do not prove singular authorship but multiple authorship must be in doubt when so much material has so much in common.

'The Denbigh Poem' has 'blest' in stanza seven and 'curst' in stanza eight. There might be an echo here of the inscription on Shakespeare's grave in Stratford, composed, it is said, by the poet himself as a warning to bone-stealers:

> *Good friend for Jesus sake forbear*
> *To dig the dust enclosed here:*
> *Blest be the man that spares these stones,*
> *And curst be he that moves my bones.*

'G' writes in stanza four, 'to wynne that grekish dame'. This same word appears in Shakespeare's *Troilus and Cressida*: I'll heat his blood with greekish wine tonight'.

'G' has an interesting use of the number ten. Stanza seven ends with, 'Blest be they all & tenne tymes blest be he', and then stanza eight repeats it, 'Curst be they all & tenne times curst be he'. Why ten? It appears in Shakespeare's Sonnet 38: 'Be thou the tenth Muse, ten times more in worth/Than those old nine which rimers invocate'.

Stanza two includes: 'The onely perle which all proud wale doth foyle' ('wale' is Wales), meaning that this man is the most attractive and valuable man in Wales (notice that the metaphor is centred on physical appearance, on aesthetic qualities). There are a number of 'pearle' in *A Midsummer Night's Dream* and the metaphor involving a foil appears in 'A Lover's Complaint': 'The foil of this false jewel'.

There does seem to be a significant degree of intertextuality between 'The Denbigh Poem' and the early work of Shakespeare. This of course does not settle the matter of authorship although it is a necessary part of a possible identification.

The reference to 'sweete philida & coridon' in stanza eleven takes us to the same pair in *A Midsummer Night's Dream* (2.1): 'And in the shape of Corin sat all day,/Playing on pipes of corn, and versing love/To amorous Phillida'. They go back to Virgil's *Seventh Eclogue*, where Corydon and Thyrsis are having a singing match. The person 'Phyllidis' does not appear before them but is referred to by Thyrsis, who compliments her by saying that when she comes, 'the woods will all rejoice in green'. Corydon replies, 'Phillis is fond of hazels'. Shakespeare changes the spellings in the play: Phyllidis becomes Phillida and Corydon becomes Corin and Coridon. The spellings are both unlike the original Virgil in the same way. 'The Denbigh Poem' uses the Shakespearean spellings.

A sonnet in the Robert Parry volume of poems by John Salusbury (numbered twenty-seven, on page 73 in the Carleton Brown volume) also invokes Coridon. This has been described in an earlier chapter.

Stanza nine of 'The Denbigh Poem' is written by 'G', who says he must leave but he apostrophises 'the muses' and tells them to 'stay ... heare'. The text implies that 'G' is an experienced writer who can pass on ('fruits of ...') his skill to John Salusbury. 'G', he says of himself, somewhat flatteringly, is a 'master' who possesses 'simple skill'. This is reminiscent of Shakespeare's *A Midsummer Night's Dream* where Quince (the organiser of plays) says: 'we come not to offend,/But with Good Will. To show our simple skill,/That is the true beginning of our end'. The writer of 'The Denbigh Poem' then flatters Salusbury again by saying that 'where e're he goe or ride/John Salusburys name shall in him bide.' The 'he ... him' is the poem's speaker whom we call 'G'.

The final stanza of section one has Salusbury dancing 'hand in hand/ treadinge the measures on the pleasant plaines'. thus dancing in a country location, consistent with Lleweni's location in the Vale of Clwyd, which at this point is a pleasant plain. Then comes the farewell: 'And thus in myddest of all this mirth and glee/I'le take my leaue of courteous Salusbury'. This reference to 'mirth and glee' is significant; it seems to refer to some special occasion in the Salusbury household. It would be explainable as a reference to a Christmas celebration, which grand houses such as Lleweni in Denbigh traditionally enjoyed, starting well before Christmas Day and sometimes extending to two or three weeks afterwards. That the speaker is leaving during this period of seasonal celebration suggests a leave-taking say in late December or some time in early January. Our next chapter turns to the second section of the poem, which is dedicated to Ursula, the high-born Stanley, the 'Phoenix'.

17

Christmas Revels: 'The Denbigh Poem': Part Two

Sally Harper, in her articles 'Shakespearean Revels' in *The New Welsh Review* (No. 56, Summer 2002) and 'Music in the Welsh Household, *c.* 1580–1620' (*Welsh History Review*), writes about a Christmas celebration at Lleweni in the 1590s.

Tucked away on the back of a leaf in a sixteenth-century manuscript kept in the University Archive at Bangor, is a fascinating list. It names thirteen poets and musicians who gathered at the great country house of Lleweni near Denbigh one Christmas during the 1590s to provide the wealthy Salusbury family with traditional-style entertainment. There are three poets..three crwth players ... and seven harpists. The heading to the list records that these 'gwyr wrth gerdd'—literally 'men of their art'—were at Lleweni during 'wilie'r natolic'—the Christmas holiday. We cannot be entirely sure in which year the gathering occurred since the final figure of the date has vanished under a worm-hole, although it may have been 1593 or 1595, as suggested by two later annotators.

Sally Harper's discovery chimes with a poem that appears in handwriting in the Christ Church Salusbury manuscript collection (included by Carleton Brown in the text section, *Poems by Sir John Salusbury, Robert Chester and others*, Christ Church MS, p. 19). Written by Robert Chester, it is not dated but is headed: 'A poore Sheapheards introduction made in A merriment of christmas at the house of the Right Worshipful John Salusbury of Lleweny Esqr Etc.' The following is extracted from its twenty-eight flattering lines:

> *Sheapheards be sylent and our musick cease*
> *heare duells our frolique friend of Arcady*
> *whose dogges defend our sheep from greedy wolues*
> *whose sheep doth cloth our silly sheapheard swaines*

whose oxen tills the grownd that yelds vs corne ...
swaines that delight in homely pleasaunt mirth
... peares Apples ...
or other fruite that this fair climatt yelds
but nipping winter and a forward spring
blasted our trees and all our sommer budds
whose blossomes shold haue yelded dainty fare
... all giftes ...
the balesome weather and cold spring denied
In signe of honor and obedience
To the whight Lyon of Arcadia ...
A homely cuntry hornpipe we will daunce
A sheapheards pretty Gigg to make him sport

We are reminded of the very poor weather of the year 1594 (and apparently 1595 was little better). This is mentioned in Robert Parry of Denbigh's diary. There are echoes of Shakespeare's language in the text: 'blasted' is especially interesting. It is found in this sense in his *The Rape of Lucrece*, 'Unruly blasts wait on the tender spring' (l.1335). This long poem, the second he dedicated to the Earl of Southampton, was registered 9 May 1594. It was probably written, according to F. E. Halliday, 'between April 1593 and May 1594' (*A Shakespeare Companion*, p. 402) All the weather allusions are reminiscent of Titania's comments in *A Midsummer Night's Dream* (Act II, Scene 2, lines 88–114):

Therefore the Winds, piping to us in vain
As in Revenge have suck'd up from the Sea
Contagious Fogs, which, falling on the land
Hath every pelting river made so proud
That they have overborne their Continents ...
The Nine-Men's-Morris is fill'd up with Mud,
And the quaint Mazes in the wanton Green,
For lack of Tread, are undistinguishable ...
The Seasons alter: hoary-headed Frosts
Fall in the fresh Lap of the crimson Rose,
And on old Hiems' chin and icy crown
An odorous chaplet of sweet Summer buds
Is as in mockery set. The Spring, the Summer,
The childing Autumn, angry Winter change
Their wonted liveries; and the mazed world
By their increase knows not which is which.

We may speculate on origins and say that the sea is some 7 miles to the north of Lleweni and that the River Clwyd runs past the walls of its farm buildings. It would be interesting to know if it originally possessed a Nine Men's Morris pitch, which is a game played outdoors on the ground.

Robert Chester was apparently a retainer in the Salusbury household. His later legal training may suggest that he had a role in estate administration. His flattering reference to his employer, John Salusbury as the 'Lion of Arcadia' is appropriate given the Salusbury emblem of the white lion. 'In sign of honour' also identifies John Salusbury as the intended recipient of Chester's flattering (and inept) lines. The allusion to dancing hand to hand, and the use of the rare term 'roundelay', are also included by 'G' in 'The Denbigh Poem'. We recall Shakespeare's 'If you will patiently daunce in our Round' (*MND*, II, 1, 140).

Sally Harper continues:

> It was commonplace for Welsh households to host gatherings of poets and musicians at Christmas ... some of the musicians must have travelled a considerable distance to reach Lleweni ... Thomas Richards, unlike the others, was a south Walian; in 1583 he played in Devon before Sir Philip Sidney.
>
> ... Consider the scene at Lleweni in the 1590's. The family and their guests would have been gathered in the great galleried hall, allegedly one of the finest medieval secular structures in Wales. Dr Johnson, visiting Lleweni with Mrs Hester Thrale (later Mrs Piozzi) in 1774, measured it meticulously, and found it to be '40 feet long and 28 broad. The Gallery 120 feet long (all paced)'. The roof rose to thirty feet. An amateur watercolour, made at some point before the hall was demolished in 1819, shows that it was panelled and fitted as an armoury, with an oak hammer-beam roof.

The timbers from this roof bear a close resemblance to those in a stone barn in the nearby farm Kilford; they could well have been salvaged and taken there, only a mile distant, during the demolition of the main part of Lleweni in 1816–1817. Dr Jonson noticed various portraits; they included one of Sir John himself, 'a half length, with short dusky hair, beardless, in a yellow figured jacket, a vast ruff, and one hand on his sword.' This was copied, as we have said, by itinerant painter Moses Griffith, and included in full colour, in an edition of Pennant's *Tour of Wales*.

Sally Harper writes:

> Two pieces in the repertory lists suggest a connection with Christmas.... But there are pieces addressed to saints with a local flavour ... [including] St Winifred of Holywell ... old style cerdd dant would surely have been part of the proceedings that Christmas at Lleweni when the ten Welsh musicians were present, but it is unlikely to have been the sum total of the

musical entertainment. Despite their Welsh roots, the Salusburies had much experience of the latest London fashions.... Most of the Lleweni tunes are specifically associated with popular dances or ballads. *Larouse, Lusty gallant* and *Al flowers of the broom* were all appropriate dances to follow a banquet, according to the Oxford-educated Nicholoas Breton (?1555–1626) writing in 1577, *Lusty gallant* was also cited as a dance by Thomas Nashe in 1595.... popular dance tunes often doubled as ballad melodies and 24 of the Lleweni items were registered ... from 1556 onwards ...

Shakespeare's works also contain references to some of the Lleweni titles: *Callino Casturame* is mentioned in *Henry V* (Act IV.sc.4); 'Can you not hit it' in *Love's Labour's Lost* (IV.1); *Light of* Love in both *Much Ado About Nothing* (111.4) and *Two Noble Kinsman* (V.2) and Peg-a-Ramsey (*Pegi Ramsdale*) in *Twelfth Night* (II.3). 'Fading' is described as a 'fine jig' in *The Winter's Tale* (IV.4).

... A further group of tunes apparently entirely unique to the Lleweni list suggests another type of entertainment within the Salusbury household. *Tarlton is buten cape* and *Tarlton trunke hose* undoubtedly refer to Richard Tarlton (d. 1588), the professional comic actor reputedly 'discovered' by a servant of the earl of Leicester at Condover in Shropshire on one of his trips to Denbigh ... There is apparently a second actor represented in the Lleweni list. *Alen his flapes* and *Alen his marche* ..refer to Edward Alleyn (1566–1626), the actor and theatre manager who later founded Dulwich College.

... Neither should we assume that households with a similar cultural outlook to that of John Salusbury invited traditional 'gwyr wrth gerdd' into their homes to play fashionable English music. Other instruments—such as fiddles and lutes—would have been better equipped to deal with that task ...

We may thus imagine the Lleweni revellers, sated with the best ales, meats and puddings ... rising to their feet. They join hands, and under the benevolent eye of their host, John Salusbury, they dance the length and breadth of the medieval hall at Lleweni until the early hours of the morning.

We now turn back to 'The Denbigh Poem', authored by 'G' (perhaps echoed in Shakespeare's 'My heart to her but as Guest-wise sojourn'd' in *A Midsummmer Night's Dream* (Act III, scene 2)). The writer says that he has 'forgott thy parte', thus using a theatrical expression. He is saying that he has written about John and excluded Ursula; now in the second part, he will write about her. He says, 'Thinke vpon her whome thou arte bound in harte/in humble duty for to recompence'. The 'thou' is John. The writer is thanking Ursula for the good time he has had in her home. The use of the terms 'duty' and 'recompense' suggest a little more than normal courtesy from one who has enjoyed the pleasures of the household. Perhaps this includes the Stanley family and their patronage. The second stanza is very specific in identifying her:

Ffrom princely blood & Ryale stocke she came
of egles brood hatcht in a loftie nest
The earle of derby & the kinge of manne
her father was her brother now possest

This clearly refers to Henry, Fourth Earl of Derby (and King of Man), as the previous holder of the title and to Ursula's brother, Ferdinando, as his successor. Henry died on 25 September 1593 and Ferdinando died on 16 April 1594. The poem must have been written between these dates. Not only can we therefore deduce the poem's composition period, we can also deduce that the writer knew Ursula and the Stanley family very well; he knew the names, the succession, the family heraldry, and their principal residence, Lathom, which was a tall, imposing, castle-like structure decorated with eagle effigies: it had an Eagle Tower and was called *The Eagle's Nest.*

If William Shakespeare was in Lancashire and Wales during the winter of 1593–1594 and the spring of 1594, he would be comparatively safe from the Plague, which was raging in London. The London theatres were closed from June 1592 to April 1594, and, as A. L. Rowse has noted, 'the plague years gave him time, away from the theatre and in the country for those ambitious compositions'. He could then have visited Flint Castle, an hour's ride from Denbigh, which would explain his familiarity with the lie of the land at Flint Castle in *Richard II* (Act III, scene 3). In the play, Bolingbroke, in a speech to Northumberland, refers to 'the grassy carpet of this plain', a true description that would be difficult to make up if one had not been there.

In this second part of 'The Denbigh Poem', Ursula and John are suitably flattered: 'so kind to her & she so kind to him ...' and in the turtle reference ('turtle-dove' symbolises constancy because the dove takes one mate for life), 'Like turtles true so doth this cuple buyld'. This, as stated earlier, links with the turtle references in *Love's Martyr* and *The Phoenix and the Turtle.*

Our particular attention is drawn to the last line, 'tho last not lest vale m[istress] Ane Stanley'. This is very peculiar. It is out of place in this poem, particularly as the final line. Suddenly in the last line the author turns to a person who has not appeared in the poem before. Even more oddly, is the 'last not least', so Anne is as important as Ursula is to 'G'.

This Anne Stanley appears to be the eldest daughter of Ferdinando, born in 1580. She would be aged thirteen–fourteen when this poem was written. Why is she mentioned here? The author says *'vale'* (goodbye) to her. Is she also at Lleweni or is she in Lancashire at one of the family homes and the author is bidding goodbye to her because he is also turning away from there? What would be special in a relationship between the person 'G', already closely linked, even if only through patronage, with John Salusbury and Ursula, and Ursula's half-brother's eldest daughter?

One explanation offers itself: that 'G' and Anne had known one another for years. A way for this to happen, given that 'G' is someone outside the family and not of a comparable class, is through a pupil-teacher relationship. We have suggested before that William Shakespeare might have worked for the Stanleys as a teacher at their households ('A Schoolmaster in the Country', Beeston) and it is possible that the teacher in this case had a special interest in his star pupil—she who was 'the fairest one of three' and had fallen for 'the learned man' (see the earlier chapter on *The Passionate Pilgrim*). She was also the eldest daughter of one who had a convincing claim to the English throne, so had a claim herself. In the final line of his encomium to John and Ursula Salusbury, the writer acknowledges the important bloodline of Anne and recalls the days when he was her teacher.

'The Denbigh Poem', as I have called it, has been subject to close linguistic analysis by Prof. David Crystal (author, with his son Ben, of the 650-page *Shakespeare's Words* (Penguin, 2002)). He calls the text of 831 words, 'The Danielle Poem'. His main purpose is to compare the words in this work with the words used in all of Shakespeare's work pre-1595. Prof. Crystal writes:

> The vocabulary of the Danielle poems is thus very much (97 percent) within what we know Shakespeare to have used at the time … On the lexical evidence, it is certainly possible that the texts could be by Shakespeare, for only a small number of usages fall outside his lexical range in 1593/4 …

This poem was written by a person who had stayed in Lleweni, Denbigh, as a guest of John and Ursula Salusbury. It expresses his appreciation and thanks for their kindness and hospitality. It is a 'thank you' script. Would such an appreciative guest, having stayed with important people, have somebody else, a copyist or scrivener, pen such a piece (as was usual with Shakespeare)? I believe not; that would be discourteous. I think he handwrote it himself.

This composition, 'The Denbigh Poem' or 'The Danielle Poem', written carefully in small, bold, clear handwriting, which appears nowhere else in the Salusbury volume, on paper of a type not elsewhere in the volume, needs to be closely considered by Shakespearean scholars. I have here detailed some of the features that lead me to believe that it could have been composed and handwritten by William Shakespeare.

18

Conclusion

So the 'lost years' have involved a long search with many blind alleys—but none, I think, are fruitless. All are revealing about his times....

Michael Wood, *In Search of Shakespeare*, p. 109

We have followed leads, as the detectives say—scores of them. We could say, as Shakespeare says in Sonnet 110, 'Alas 'tis true, I have gone here and there,/ And made myself a motley to the view'. The 'motley' will depend on the reader's perception. The future will decide, sooner or later—probably later. Some pointers and some assertions will turn out to be in the right direction, and correct, some in the wrong direction, and wrong. This is a prime area for literary sleuthing, and it should continue.

Sonnet 33's haunting phrase 'stealing unseen' can be well applied to Shakespeare's life (what little of it we know) in the period 1578–1592.

We can understand the lack of reliable biographical data through the life's first fourteen years or so because Shakespeare was just another small boy in a provincial town, belonging to an undistinguished family. Yet at the watershed time, when he left school and the flower of his genius started to open, the lack of information begins to seem more wilful than circumstantial. His father's Catholicism would have caused him to be cautious, wary of revealing his name and his origins. If his Catholic origins were known, it would put him in the wrong company at least, and at most, in fear of his life. Another significant reason for his being 'unseen' would be the poor financial state of his parents and siblings in Stratford (and of his own wife and children before he started making substantial sums of money out of theatre in London after March 1592). His parents, especially his father, because of their comparative poverty, would have lost much of their local social status; this was a matter of shame (and perhaps the 'disgrace' of the sonnets); consequently, any advancement in life by William would be accompanied by a necessary reticence about his name and family background.

Of course, he was a social climber; he had to be. Success in creative activities at that time depended to a large extent on patronage. He moved towards the sources of patronage and behaved accordingly. He was driven by ambition, by a desire to prove himself—that a boy from an ordinary family from the market town of Stratford could perform, behave, create, and achieve as well as anybody: those better educated graduates of the universities and the privileged upper classes with their private tutors, income, books, superior accommodation, and connections.

He was driven by artistic ambition: to prove that he could create artefacts which were as fine as if not finer than anything being then produced. One extraordinary thing about Shakespeare is the way he held the commercial and the aesthetical together. He hardly wrote a word that was not useful for some practical purpose: to attract a patron, to please someone, to entertain a fee-paying audience and encourage them to return to the theatre to see more of his work, to create his name as a writer and poet (a higher position than 'playwright'), to make money so that he could invest it in land and property, and so on. He combined this utilitarian proceeding (causing much envy among his peers) with the creation of work so fine, so exalted (and so popular) as has never been surpassed in the history of the literature of the world.

So, he moved forward and upward, away from his humble origins, leaving his home setting, then utilising it in his work. There is hardly any aspect of workaday Stratford in the mid- and late sixteenth century that does not in some way appear in Shakespeare's plays. That huge output includes much that has puzzled commentators. They question how a little-educated commoner could know so much, and how he knew so much of the ways of the nobility. We have tried to supply part of an answer in the foregoing pages, in presenting the Lancashire Theory through oblique supporting detail, so that it presents itself as coherent and 'very possible'. His knowledge of the classics and history came largely through his talent for 'gutting' books for the material he wanted; those books were available through the support of friends and patrons, especially through the libraries of noble families. His knowledge of the daily lives of the nobility came from his having lived with them, in the same household. His quiet, systematic association with individuals of knowledge and culture brought its rewards in understanding, attitude, and good judgement.

The foregoing chapters have gathered information in relation to the puzzle of his 'missing years' and offered a possible solution. We have pointed to the history plays and asked why these were written in such a sequence and why they were written early in his writing career. Their presentation of the Lancastrian line is clear, as is the bias towards the Lancastrians, the Stanleys (see the discussion of the presentation of the Battle of Bosworth), and the Tudors. The great poet Edmund Spenser was well informed and clearly mentions Shakespeare's association with the outstanding theatrical patron, Ferdinando, Fifth Earl of

Derby. Two precious volumes appear in our narrative, Halle's *Chronicle* and Plutarch's *Lives*: the former possibly containing Shakespeare's handwriting, the annotations having a clear link with the history plays; the latter, a source of many stories and characters in the plays, once in the possession of the Derbys and for a significant period owned, tantalisingly, by a 'William'. The Plutarch volume could also feature Shakespeare's handwriting, including a downward looped scribble.

We have followed a putative biographical trail, starting with a Lancastrian schoolteacher in Stratford, then going up to Lea, near Preston, where an ageing nobleman dictated his will and directed that one of his favourite retainer—'William Shakeshafte'—should be employed by a 'good master'. That trail came down the spine of Lancashire, through Rufford, to Lathom, near Ormskirk, the home (with Knowsley, some ten miles further south) of the hugely wealthy and influential Stanley family.

Possible Lancastrian imagery and language have been identified in Shakespeare's work, utilising the exact and modest work of the late Clifford Broadbent.

A young Welsh nobleman, John Salusbury, has been brought in to our narrative. It is suggested that he had a much more prominent part in Shakespeare's life than has previously been thought. This writer believes there were three significant young noblemen who appear as faceless images in Shakespeare's sonnets and that John Salusbury (as Frances Keen said) might well have been one of them. John's wife, Ursula, was brought up at Hawarden Castle, which our narrative suggests could be the setting of Shakespeare's long poem *A Lover's Complaint*.

In the library of Christ Church, Oxford, there is an ancient bound volume comprising the Salusbury Papers. On two leaves, in distinctive handwriting, is what I have called 'The Denbigh Poem'. This describes John Salusbury and his wife in glowing terms, says that the writer visited their home in Denbigh, finishing with a greeting to a certain Anne Stanley (spelt in the poem 'Ane'). The poem exhibits dozens of Shakespearean characteristics in its imagery and themes. It contains words which, according to the respected linguistic scholar Prof. David Crystal, are those typically used by Shakespeare at the time.

All the above features are potentially coherent. They can be seen as part of a narrative. Time and place fit in to a possible over-all pattern. In this book, I have identified this pattern and placed its details before the reader.

In selecting material, I have proceeded according to a method which can be described as 'intelligent inference'.

Finally, we observe that behind the rise of Shakespeare in the sixteenth and seventeen centuries is the rise of England—its statehood and its economy—and the English language, through the previous four centuries or so. Outlining these two major themes has been beyond the scope of this book. But no extraordinary individual rises in a vacuum. The England of Elizabeth was a period unlike any other in British History. It was fast-moving, unpredictable, self-confident, and proud. It had bravery and high-achievement; it sent adventurers in small ships thousands of miles across a huge ocean to discover America, and they usually returned. It marked the end of an old order in many ways and the beginning of a new. It was the breeding ground of our modern democracy, of our economy, our civic and state procedures, and of our Arts.

The success of the British state is tied in with the success of the English language. It is one of the newest of the five thousand or so languages on the planet. It started as the tongue of people living in central England, including Stratford-upon-Avon, developed swiftly in areas around the Thames, especially in London, and in a few hundred years, accompanied by the success of the British state, its versatility and suppleness—exploited and altered by Shakespeare and other Elizabethan writers—endowed it with such range, vigour and beauty that, only some four hundred years later, it is the *lingua franca* of the world.

However, back to our central theme: where was Shakespeare? The 'missing years' are still the missing years. It is a mystery. Yet it is capable of being solved. What we need, finally, is 'hard evidence'. Some dusty corner of a library or some old box containing family papers might produce a document with Shakespeare's name on it, implying that he was at 'X' with 'Y' on such-and-such a date. Another 'find' might be an official list of taxable persons or creditors with his name on it. Some old book, possibly with Lancastrian origins, might be at this moment be sitting on a shelf, unnoticed, containing an annotation indicating Shakespeare's presence in a place at a certain time. A newly discovered Elizabethan letter might contain a reference to him. Our present book might help to raise awareness in this area so that when new material does emerge, its significance can be better identified and understood.

Facsimile of
'The Denbigh Poem'

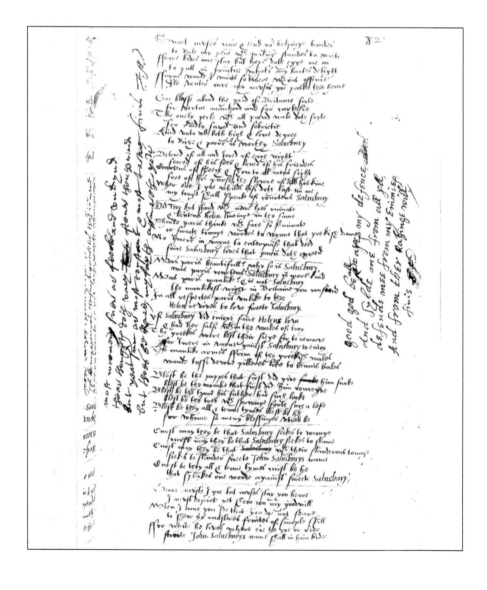

Opposite: The first page of 'The Denbigh Poem' from the Christ Church Salusbury Volume.

Below middle: The second page of 'The Denbigh Poem' from the Chrirst Church Salusbury Volume.

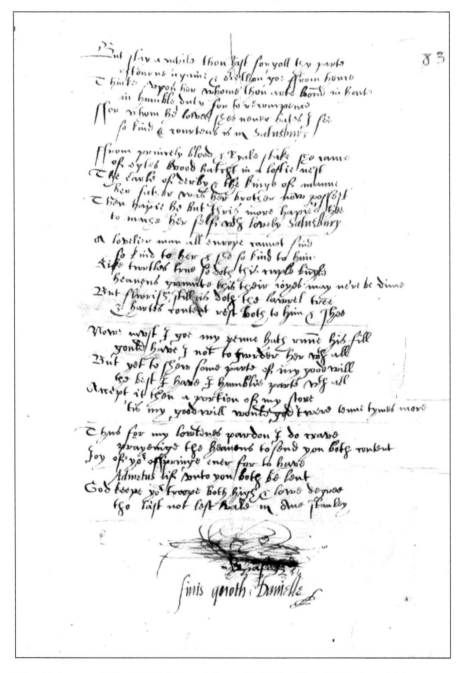

The third page of 'The Denbigh Poem' from the Christ Church Salusbury Volume.

APPENDIX II

Typescript of 'The Denbigh Poem'

XXI.

Sweet mvses come & lend your helpinge handes   [fol. 82]
    to Rule my penne which quakinge standes to write
ffeare bides me stay but hope doth egge me on
    to putt in practize what's my hartes delight
ffayne would I write so 'twere without offence
    I'le venter once my mvse goe packe thee hence

Goe blasse abrod the prid of Britance soyle
    for vertue manhood and for curtesie
The onely perle which all prowd wale doth foyle
    for kindly favour and sobrietie
Kind vnto all both high & lowe degree
    to Riche & poore is worthy S a l u s b u r y

Beloued of all and Ioyed of each wight
    scared of his foes & loued of his friendes
Courteus of speech & show to all mens sight
    free of his purse, the flowre of all his kine
Wher e're I goe whiles lif doth last in me
    my tonge shall speake of courteus S a l u s b u r y

Did Troy but stand which nowe lyes ruinate
    & beauteus helen liueinge in the same
Should paris thinke with face so feminate
    or smooth tounge wordes to wynne that grekish dame
No 'twere in vayne to enterprise that deed
    since S a l u s b u r y lives that paris doth exceed.

Was paris beautifull? why so is S a l u s b u r y ,
    was paris courteus?   S a l u s b u r y is more kind
Was paris manlike? & is not S a l u s b u r y
    the manlikest wight in Britaine you can find
In all respectes paris vnlike to thee
    Helen revives to love sweete S a l u s b u r y

Yf S a l u s b u r y did enioye faire Helens love
    & had her salf within the wales of troy
The greekes were best their siege for to remoove
    for 'twere in vayne gainst S a l u s b u r y to enioy
His manlike armes ffrom of the greekish wales
    would tosse downe pilleres like to tennis bales

Blest be the pappes that first did give him sucke
    blest be the wombe that first did him conceyve
Blest be they all & tenne tymes blest be he
    blest be the tree which sprwnge forth [1] such a lefe
Blest be they all & tenne tymes blest be he
    for whome so meny blessinges vtred be

Curst may they be that S a l u s b u r y seekes to wronge
    curst may they be that S a l u s b u r y seekes to shame
Curst may they be that with their slanderous tounge
    seekes to slander sweete J o h n S a l u s b u r y s name
Curst be they all & tenne tymes curst be he
    that speakes one worde against sweete S a l u s b u r y

Hence mvste I goe but mvses stay you heare
    I mvst departe yet shew you my goodwill
When I ame gon see that you doe not feare
    to shew your masteres fruites of simple skill
ffor while he lives where e're he goe or ride
    sweete J o h n S a l u s b u r y s name shall in him bide

[1] Ms. fouth.

Denbighe adew pray thou for S a l u s b u r y   [fol. 82ᵇ]
   north wales adew pray ye for S a l u s b u r y
The sweetest gemme that cures *your* melencolie
   is kind & faire & courteus S a l u s b u r y
Pray you for him & I will pray for yee
   so god blesse vs & courteus S a l u s b u r y

Nowe mvses stay I may no longer write
   to drolle ame I to speake of S a l u s b u r y prais
Some finer wittes hearafter shall indite
   & putt his name in coridons roondelays
Then sweete philida & coridon agree
   to singe in prays of lovinge S a l u s b u r y

And I'le intreat dianas trayne to stand
   to lend ye help with all their siluer stringes
The nimphes shall dance with S a l u s b u r y hand in hand
   treadinge the measures on the pleasant plaines
And thus in myddest of all his mirth & glee
   I'le take my leaue of courteus S a l u s b u r y
         finis quoth Danielle.

XXII.

But stay a while thou hast forgott thy parte   [fol. 83ᵃ]
   retourne againe & ere thou goe ffrom hence
Thinke vpon her whome thou arte bound in harte
   in humble duty for to recompence
ffor whom he loves shee neuer hates I see
   so kind & courteus is m[istress] S a l u s b u r y

ffrom princely blood & Ryale stocke she came
   of egles brood hatcht in a loftie nest
The earle of derby & the kinge of manne
   her father was her brother now possest
Then hapie he but thris more hapie's shee
   to mache her self with lovely S a l u s b u r y

A lovelier man all europe cannot find
   so kind to her & she so kind to him
Like turtles true so doth this cuple buyld
   heauens graunte this their ioyes may ne're be dim
But flwrish still as doth the lawrel tree
   & hartes content rest both to him & shee

Nowe mvst I goe my penne hath runne his fill
   gould have I not to gwrder [1] her with all
But yet to shew some parte of my good will
   the best I have I humblie parte with all
Accept it then a portion of my store
   'tis my good will would god 'twere tenne tymes mor

Thus for my bowldnes pardon I do crave
   prayeinge the heauens to send you both content
Ioy of *your* ofspringe euer for to have
   A d m e t u s lif vnto you both be lent
God keepe *your* troope both high & lowe degree
   tho last not lest vale m[istress] Ane stanley
         finis quoth Danielle

Bibliography

Ackroyd, P., *Tudors* (Pan, 2012); *Shakespeare: The Biography* (Vintage, 2006)

Booth, S. (ed.) *Shakespeare's Sonnets* (Yale University Press, 2000)

Boyce, C., *Encyclopedia of Shakespeare* (Roundtable Press, 1990)

Burgess, A., *Shakespeare* (Penguin, 1917)

Cambrensis, G., *Itinerary through Wales*, trans. R. C. Hoare (Everyman Dent, 1976)

Chambers, E. K., *William Shakespeare: A Study in Facts and Problems, Vols 1 and 2* (Oxford University Press, 1930); *Elizabethan Gleanings* (Oxford University Press, 1944)

Cooper, T., *Searching for Shakespeare* (National Portrait Gallery, 2006)

Cross, W. L., and Brooke, T. (eds), *The Yale Shakespeare* (Barnes and Noble, 1993)

Crystal, D., and Crystal, B., *Shakespeare's Words* (Penguin, 2002)

Dawson, G. E., and Kennedy-Skipton, L., *Elizabethan Handwriting 1500–1650* (Phillimore & Co Ltd, 1981)

Duncan-Jones, K., (ed.) *Shakespeare's Sonnets* (Arden, 1997)

Duncan-Jones, K., and Woudhuysen, H. R. (eds), *Shakespeare's Poems* (Arden, 2007)

Duncan-Jones, K., *Ungentle Shakespeare* (Arden, 2001)

George, D., 'The Playhouse at Prescot and the 1572–3 Plague', in *Region, Religion and Patronage; Lancastrian Shakespeare* (Manchester University Press, 2003)

Gidman, J. M., *Sir William Stanley of Holt* (Rosalba Press, 2003)

Greenblatt, S., *Will in the World* (Jonathan Cape, 2004)

Halliday, F. E., *Shakespeare* (Thames and Hudson, 1964); *A Shakespeare Companion 1564–1964* (Penguin, 1964)

Hamilton, C., *In Search of Shakespeare* (Robert Hale, 1986)

Harpur, S., 'Music in the Welsh Household *c.* 1580–1620', *Welsh History Review* Issue 21 No. 4

Harries, F. J., *The Welsh in Shakespeare* (Fisher Unwin, 1919)

Hinman, C., *The Norton Facsimile of the First Folio of Shakespere* (Hamlyn, 1955)

Holden, A., *William Shakespeare: His Life and Work* (Abacus, 1999)

Honan, P., *Shakespeare a Life* (Oxford University Press, 1988)

Honigmann, E. A. J., *Shakespeare: The 'Lost Years'* (Manchester University Press, 1985)

Hubbard, E., *CLWYD* (Penguin, 1986)

Hughes, H. E., *Eminent Men of Denbighshire* (Brython Press, 1942)

Jones, J. I., 'William Shakespeare and John Salusbury', *Denbighshire Historical Society Transactions*, Vol. 59, 2011

Keen, A., and Lubbock, R., *The Annotator* (Putnam, 1954)

Kermode, F., *Shakespeare's Language* (Penguin, 2001)

Kerrigan, J. (ed.), *William Shakespeare: The Sonnets and A Lover's Complaint* (Penguin, 1986)

Knight, G. W., *The Mutual Flame* (Methuen, 1955)

Lee, S., *A Life of William Shakespeare* (Murray, 1916)

Levi, P., *The Life and Times of William Shakespeare* (Macmillan, 1988)

New Welsh Review Nos 23, 25, and 56

Nichol, C., *Shakespeare and his Contemporaries* (National Portrait Gallery, 2005); *The Lodger: Shakespeare on Silver Street* (Penguin, 2007)

Owen, M., *A Grand Tour of North Wales* (Gwasg Carreg Gwalch, 2003)

Pollard, A. W. (ed.), *Shakespeare's Hand in the Play of Sir Thomas More* (Cambridge University Press, 1920)

Prince, F. T. (ed.), *The Poems* (Methuen, 1960)

Roberts, E., 'Ymryson y Salsbriaid 1593', *Denbighshire Historical Society Transactions*, Vol. 17, 1968

Robinson, J. M., *A Guide to the Country Houses of the North-West* (Constable, 1991)

Rowse, A. L., *The England of Elizabeth* (Macmillan, 1955); *William Shakespeare: A Biography* (Macmillan, 1963)

Salter, M., *The Castles of North Wales* (Folly Publications, 1997)

Salusbury, Sir J., Chester, R., and Brown, C. (intr.), *Poems by Sir John Salusbury and Robert Cheste* (Bryn Mawr, 1913)

Sams, E. (ed.), *Shakespeare's Edmund Ironside* (Wildwood House, 1985); (ed.) *Shakespeare's Edward III* (Yale University Press, 1996)

Sams, E., *The Real Shakespeare: Retrieving the Early Years 1564–1594* (Yale University Press, 1995)

Schoenbaum, S., *Willliam Shakespeare: A Compact Documentary Life* (Oxford University Press, 1978); *William Shakespeare: A Documentary Life* (Oxford Scholar Press, 1975)

Shakespeare, W., *A Midsummer Night's Dream* (ed. Harold F. Brooks) (Arden, 1979); (eds Quiller-Couch, A., and Wilson, J. D.) (Cambridge University Press, 1924)

Shapiro, J., *1599: A Year in the Life of William Shakespeare* (Faber & Faber, 2005)

Smith, K., *Shakespeare and Son* (Praeger, 2011)

Thurley, S., *The Royal Palaces of Tudor England* (Yale University Press, 1993)

Wilson, I., *Shakespeare: The Evidence* (Headline, 1993)

Wilson, J. D., *Life in Shakespeare's England: A Book of Elizabethan Prose* (Cambridge University Press, 1926); *The Essential Shakespeare* (Cambridge University Press, 1943)

Wilson, R., *Secret Shakespeare* (Manchester University Press, 2004)

Wood, M., *In Search of Shakespeare* (BBC, 2003)